Choose You

Kay Sibson

Copyright © 2026 Kayla Sibson, writing as Kay Sibson. All rights reserved. Published by Novapricity, LLC.

This book is a work of creative nonfiction. While it draws on personal experiences and reflections, names and identifying details have been changed where needed to protect privacy.

No part of this publication may be reproduced, stored, or shared in any format or medium, including electronic or mechanical methods, without prior written permission from the publisher or author, except for brief quotations used in reference.

This work may not be used, in whole or in part, to train, develop, or refine artificial intelligence systems, machine learning models, datasets, or similar technologies. This includes any use for data extraction or model input. Such use is not permitted.

Disclaimer: This book reflects personal experience and perspective and is not a substitute for professional mental health or medical support. What I share here reflects what would have supported me, offered as perspective. Take what's helpful and leave the rest.

ISBNs
Print/Paperback: 979-8-9923289-1-2
EBook: 979-8-9923289-2-9

Cover Illustration by Alexandra Love

Interior Illustrations by Alexandra Love

Interior Layout by Golden Editorial LLC

Editing by Golden Editorial LLC

Printed in the United States of America

First Edition

To my younger self: Be loud, feel it all, and pick the pink one.

Like a tree standing right where it is,
just being here for these few moments is enough.

Contents

1

Choose Your Own Unfolding

I've spent most of my life trying to change who I am. For the better part of my childhood and adolescence, I believed I was a problem to fix. Looking back, I can see how my role as the oldest daughter of five, raised in the Christian religion, planted and nurtured that idea. The constant messaging of media, society, and its systems reinforced these thoughts at every turn. The sense that I was broken may have come from things outside me, maybe from the "strong work ethic" my dad instilled in me, but I believed it, and I took fixing myself very seriously.

I filled my free time reading more books, praying harder, and shaming, guilting, and punishing myself to improve and change who I was with the hope of being happy. Most of the books on my nightstand, paired with my self-criticism, only made me feel further from who I should be and how my life should feel. It was an endless cycle of corrections to be made as I pushed to achieve my goals. While I think we can always find ways to improve, I was operating through the lens that I had to be less me to be successful or at peace.

I thought once I fixed myself, things would feel and be easier to manage. I felt I had to change who I was to change my life.

Over time, instead of improving and feeling more secure, I abandoned myself almost altogether. I ignored my body, my emotions, and the whispers that tried to call me back to who I was. I was the embodiment of a tug-of-war between heart and mind. My feelings and thoughts strained between feeling restless and feeling a numbness I mistook for peace.

Eventually, I found my shelves filled with self-help books and journals as I documented my self-improvement journey. I thought that by seeking to improve, I was learning more about myself and how to be better. Sure, maybe I learned more ways to analyze, label, and mentally connect the dots, but I didn't truly meet myself. I could tell you all the basic facts of who I was, why things came about, why I made a decision, or what happened, but I avoided connecting with who I was on a deep level. I didn't know what I wanted, and I didn't understand the essence of who I was, so I shut down. I had to be a better version of me before I could embrace and love myself.

In my early 20s, I met my now-husband. I didn't realize this at the time, but it was my relationship with him and his love for me that changed the trajectory of my life. I never viewed him as perfect, but I knew he was perfect for me; exactly what I needed. From the very beginning, one of the most important things he gave me was space to be me. There was never a point in our relationship when he suggested, directly or indirectly, that I needed to change for us to be happy together. That was a brand-new experience for me.

There is this idea that we need to change who we are or our situation to become our true selves. What if, instead of trying to change who we are to grow, we choose to connect more deeply with who we already are? All the close relationships I had previously involved me morphing into someone else to make that person feel secure, loved, or whatever it was they thought was my responsibility. Because he neither asked nor need me to change, I was able to pause my chameleon behavior and exist as exactly who I was. This pause opened a door and a question I began to consider: What if I was *more* me instead of less?

At 27, a couple of years into our marriage, I saw my life through clear eyes for the first time. Some call it a "quarter-life crisis," and while it was confronting, I wouldn't call it a crisis. I stepped back far enough to see where I was headed and decided I needed to pivot. So much change had occurred around me, and I didn't know how to handle it or adjust to it. At work, I had stepped into an upper management role, taking on more responsibility without the pay increase to match, and I realized I didn't actually support the company's vision. I began seeing unhealthy or limiting patterns in my relationship with my parents. I noticed I wasn't as open as I thought I was, quietly holding back parts of myself and what mattered to me. And I was uncertain what I was working toward at all. I couldn't see how the life I was living connected to the goals I thought I had, or if those goals were even truly mine. I wasn't sure I could go down a new path even if I found one. What was happening in my life was beyond my control, and I was exhausted. I realized I wasn't being true to who I was in relationships, in my pursuits, and in how I was showing up in the world. It wasn't that I was lying about who I was; I had become disconnected from myself. I didn't fully know who I was underneath everything, and at the same time, I didn't feel safe to be myself, even with myself. I had to shift my focus away from change and instead focus on growth.

I see change and growth as two different things. Change, for me and in this book, is the life, events, and experiences that happen around and outside of us. It's the natural progression of things, the unknown, and the unexpected. It's external—the situations we find ourselves in, how things look, the things that happen to us—all of which represent forms of change. Change is not inherently good or bad; it's simply what unfolds as we live. When we pursue or experience change, it looks and feels like movement; if we desire the change, it feels like progress. Generally, if we don't desire the change, it feels like a stall or like we are moving backward. Change can reroute us, take us places we never thought of, and influence us internally.

Growth, on the other hand, is internal. Growth is how we respond to or connect with change, our lives, and the people around us. It's how we feel and how we interact with who we are in relation to where we are. It may look like a pause or slower progress, but it doesn't mean there is a lack of movement. Growth is the development and evolution of us. Maybe you're like me and, at some point, narrowed or confused your own view of growth, thinking that you or your situation had to change before growth could happen. But we can grow more of who we are not by changing, but by nurturing what's already here. I don't see growth as working to improve who we are, but rather as supporting how we feel and helping us live as more of who we are. By focusing on our growth, we can learn, expand, and adapt in health and balance. Without awareness of where we are and our growth, we can stretch ourselves thin, deplete ourselves, and become rigid. We may also limit our capacity and feel uncomfortable being who we are.

For example, change may look like being laid off and being forced to find a new job, whereas a form of growth is seeking a new career or position that feels like a better fit, or taking a course to deepen your skill set. Growth can also look like building better relationships within your current position, so work feels more connected and enjoyable. Growth doesn't always reflect or result in an outward change in our lives. Focusing on external change often centers on how things look and can leave us waiting for change to happen before we feel better. It becomes something we respond to when it arrives. Focusing on internal growth shifts how we feel as change is happening. It allows us to be where we are while still moving forward. It's the difference between waiting for your circumstances to change before you feel secure and learning how to feel more at ease within them while they are still unfolding. We can't outrun change or circumstances, but we can feel better within them and be ready for whatever may come.

When we spend too much time focusing on change, things we only have so much influence over, we run the risk of disconnecting from how we feel and our core selves. Our situation can feel imbalanced, fragile against strong winds, or confined. Daily tasks can feel harder, and even things we used to enjoy start to feel taxing. In our effort to improve, we can end up ignoring what's already here and disengage from our center. Growth is about revealing more you, more of what's already inside, not becoming someone new. There's nothing you need to change. Growing is about self-discovery—a deepening relationship with yourself—or self-recovery when needed. I thought I wanted and needed to change who I was so my life would change into how I envisioned it, but what I ultimately wanted was my growth to happen alongside change.

So, in order to grow, to be more of who I was within my life and its circumstances, I had to stop trying to change and instead be myself. I needed to remember who that was. I needed to cultivate a safe space so I could pause, look at where I was and discover which pieces I was working with, and begin to connect with them. Growth requires stabilization. Growth can happen naturally with and through us by focusing on what's been within us all along. We must embrace all of who we are and what has shaped us.

Growth is a relationship and what develops over time and experience. It's not something to rush or achieve. We are human beings; we are not fixed or stationary. We are always participating, always in motion as long as we live. Sustainable growth is about gaining and maintaining a self-perception of who and where we are. It's staying present and allowing ourselves to be who we are, regardless of our circumstances.

When we are working towards our goals, some of us can fixate too much on the outcome, to the point of ignoring who we are right now. I'm not talking about the effort to adjust or add healthy habits to our daily lives. I'm talking about the way we seem to require ourselves, or our lives, to fit perfectly into a box or under a label we have deemed worthy or good enough. We can be overly critical and demanding of ourselves when we don't live up to the ideal in our heads. In our effort to improve, we separate from ourselves. We don't need more judgment; instead, we need more relationships; so we can grow to be more of what makes us who we are.

For over ten years of my life, I dedicated myself to self-improvement and healing to find peace and ease. In that time, I tried more tools and techniques than I can list, from various forms of therapy and energy work to books, classes, and both Eastern and Western practices. Over time, I added tools and resources to my metaphorical "Emotional & Mental Support Toolbox" and found ways to use them that work for me. That's not to say I have it all figured out or that I never need additional help or support.

No one taught me how to connect and know myself. Many people and resources lead with basic frameworks, strengths and weaknesses questionnaires, labels, or even using things like our birth date as one way to understand who we are. These can be helpful tools, but they don't tell the whole story. What I found and used to connect with myself were not things I could complete once and consider done. They are tools to explore and play with, not something to complete or check off. The reflections and practices I share in this book come from that toolbox and are things I still use today. They help me return to my center and stay true to who I am, no matter what comes. This book is not meant to be a crutch. It is a starting point. The exercises and reflections are meant to spark ideas and give you somewhere to begin. It is flexible enough to return to when you want a reminder or encouragement to discover something more about what is coming up for you.

There are many paths someone might take to connect and get to know themselves better. Here I'm sharing what worked best for me and the lenses through which I approach them. Part of me once thought it would be easier if there was one path. But it wasn't one method, one tool, or one moment when I found security within myself. It happened over time and in my own way. It was all the moments I showed up for myself and connected to who I was. It was through an honest and close relationship with myself that I found my current internal baseline of calm and curiosity.

There's no shortage of self-improvement advice, guidance on achieving more, and instructions for how to change where and who you are. This book is a reminder that it's safe to be who you are, as you are, and guides you on a journey to discovering how to connect with who that is. It's a way to remember, acknowledge, and embrace your feelings, your past, the parts of yourself that you've hidden or tried to change. It's a way to make space for more possibilities and unfolding in whatever way that looks and means to you. These practices keep me meeting myself where I am. They stay with me because they work again and again, not because I haven't grown, but because they grow with me. You may discover your own versions along the way as you continue to unfold into more of yourself.

If you're feeling lost in your relationship to yourself or struggling to feel at ease with who you are, this book offers a way to reflect and connect with those aspects of you, so you may be able to continue your journey with greater steadiness, greater ease, and more play. By choosing you, you choose to connect with your needs and wants. When you know them, you can respond and act in alignment with them. You gain your own sense of stability and clarity, enabling you to choose better for yourself and stay present. When we feel safe, we feel more ease and space to be who we are and live life the way we want.

This book is for those who want to feel more secure, whether they are expanding or have just experienced a season of expansion and now desire to find their balance again. It's for those who are tired of self-improvement and want to practice simply being where and who they are. This book focuses on the stability aspect of growth and discovering more of who you are. Reflecting and harmonizing within change and expansion; being rather than doing. Your intention and awareness don't have to be about controlling or changing who you are, your situation, or your past. They can be about choosing to meet yourself: who you are at your core, your feelings, your history, your beliefs, and your wants and needs.

By the end of this book, you will be able to practice cultivating inner safety to continue exploring who you are and your relationship with yourself. Using different lenses, we will explore, reflect on, and practice connecting with various aspects of ourselves. What comes from being in relationship with who we are is the ability to sustain, grow, and respond to life's unknowns with calm. To be more of yourself with yourself, in your relationships, decisions, actions, and to know yourself on a deeper level. To know not just your past and all the things that shape you, but to know how to support who you are and how you're expanding.

Choosing you is about coming into a relationship with ourselves, our bodies, and our feelings to find our center and know ourselves more deeply. Choosing you is companionship with yourself. It's connecting on different levels, not a correction of self. When you choose to be in relationship with yourself, rather than a product of your circumstances, you're choosing to be a participant in your unfolding. Choose to connect with who and where you are, not because there isn't room to grow, but so you *can* grow.

2
Seasons

I was sitting with my back against a large pine tree on a spring day. It was sunny and peaceful as the smell of pine filled my lungs, and the tears fell over my cheeks. I sighed in surrender. I had been miserable, but unwilling to admit it to myself. I had felt frozen in my circumstances, but I wasn't trapped; I had options, too many of them, and I didn't know how or which way to continue. I could continue on the trajectory I was on, working the way I was. I could pivot my business to make more sense for me. I could go back to school or take courses to develop a new aspect of my work, or do something new altogether. I had an idea of the future I wanted, but I was getting confused, trying to figure out what would feel best and work for me.

Growth and self-development had been a driving force, almost an obsession, for most of my life, and at this point, it had been over two years of working on expanding myself and my life. Within that time, I quit my corporate job to start my own business, and in doing so, I learned new skills, put myself out there, worked with new clients and people, taught workshops, and did podcast interviews. I thought all of that effort to propel my career forward would look and feel different than it did right then. I had strategies, infrastructure, and everything looked right on paper, but how it was playing out in front of me wasn't working.

I was both depressed and anxious, and spent most days feeling a sense of fear that I was going to miss the opportunity that would make everything finally make sense. It wasn't just about money—though I needed more—it was a sense of stability that I thought reaching specific goals would bring me. So I kept pushing, kept doing more to find that sense of ease I had hoped would come eventually. I did my best to ignore the feelings of doubt and uncertainty pressing in on me.

From waking up to going to bed at night, I was either rushing to get through the discomfort of my reality, checking off items on my to-do list, or avoiding them altogether. The further I went, the more I separated from myself and how I was feeling. I pretended everything was fine, so maybe things would be, but it got harder and harder to keep going. I struggled to feel satisfaction in my work and remember what I was working toward.

I didn't want to acknowledge that what I had been building the last two years would break at the first test of strength, or that I might break with it. I had outer stability, like tools and systems, prepared and able to take on expansion. But I was struggling to find inner stability, a sense of safety within myself in relation to the expansion

I had experienced. Logically, I knew what was wrong, that I was off balance, but I hadn't wanted to confront or confirm it.

For months, I felt this pull and subtle nudges to acknowledge parts of me I had neglected, ignored, or hadn't yet seen. Intellectually, I knew myself. I had spent years trying to uncover as much as I could about myself. But when it came to truly knowing my inner world—the kind of understanding that can only come from experience—I had put my relationship with myself on the back burner in pursuit of my goals. I thought that when I reached the next milestone, I would come back and reconnect with myself again. I had been waiting to feel secure in my work and circumstances to be in a relationship with myself.

Much of my life was dedicated to searching for security, solid foundations, and structures to keep me stable, ready for anything. I believed that if I found stability, I would find ease. I could be myself and be free to live and show up however I wanted. I spent many years looking to things and people outside of myself for answers. I wrestled to find safety in people, my accomplishments, work, and money. All of it only led to temporary feelings of safety. It was only when I nurtured it within myself that it remained steady.

It was in that moment, leaning against that strong, stable tree, that I allowed myself to feel, to recognize how removed I had been from myself, from what I wanted, and what I needed. I took a few deep breaths. I gave myself enough space to simply be, and I met who was there. I admitted to myself how tired I had been, pushing myself to grow to reach a new height, and I wondered if, instead, I could be more like this tree.

Trees are simply themselves. They don't change what type of tree they are, they just grow, sustainably and in their own time. I needed something to shift in my favor, but I couldn't wait for change or for conditions to be perfect before making new choices. I remembered that my relationship with myself in the present moment was the key to feeling secure, no matter what I was experiencing in my life.

So I gave myself time to reconnect to who I was, got honest with myself, and started reflecting on my present life and season. Honesty with ourselves is the foundation of self-discovery and growth. If we don't have a relationship with ourselves built on honesty, it's hard to stay intact, to stay with who we are while navigating change. Honesty helps us maintain balance and clarity about how we are doing and what direction we are heading. When it comes to establishing or maintaining that openness, looking at where we are right now is a great place to start. We can look at who is here today, how we are showing up, and what our current situation looks like. We don't have to rely on or wait for change to experience more growth.

In that time of reevaluation, I started to understand something about growth: expansion is what we often focus on—reaching new goals, changing careers, learning new skills, building or creating more. I believe our society and our culture add pressure to change and expand who we are: to produce more and be a specific version of self. This makes growth seem like something to attain. While self-expansion isn't inherently negative—changing unhealthy habits is a meaningful form of growth—I belive growth can also take place naturally over time.

Growth isn't just expansion, or something new, or bigger, or better; it's an evolution of who we are at our core. Expansion is only one aspect of growth. All expansion needs adequate, proportional stability to maintain it. There's a lot of information and resources about growth that focus on expansion and doing more, but as we expand, we also need stability to be able to hold that expansion. When we are too focused on expanding and change, we may disconnect from ourselves and struggle to find and keep our balance.

Both expansion and stabilization can occur internally and externally, on both large and small scales. Outward expansion may look obvious, like buying a house or taking a new step in your relationship. Inward expansion can look like learning a new skill or surpassing a personal record. Often, we focus more on expanding ourselves, our businesses, and our lives. We say yes to new ideas, take on new responsibilities, or work toward bigger goals. We invest more of our resources to reach new levels. It may look like the fruits of our labor coming in, seeing our hard work pay off, or finally being able to start something new in our lives. Other times, our circumstances may require us to expand our capabilities in ways we didn't seek out or plan for. We may suddenly need to take care of a loved one, our car breaks down, or our responsibilities at work shift, and we're pressed to adapt the best we can.

Outer stability can come from having enough time, money, and resources, allowing our basic needs to be met. Inner stability is about our connection to ourselves: how well we know and respond to ourselves, and our ability to care for our inner world when our outer world is unpredictable. It's reflecting and processing, meeting what's within. It's feeling our feelings as they show up. It's being the most expressed version of ourselves.

Sustainable unfolding relies on your relationship with yourself and your ability to meet what arises. When we know and connect with ourselves, we can find inner grounding. This inner stability allows us to see ourselves and our experiences more clearly. In deepening our relationship with ourselves, we grow not by forcing or striving toward our goals, but by engaging with and being more of who we are. Lasting growth requires stability to support our expansion and a functional relationship between the two. When we work toward growth, expansion can happen, but if we aren't rooted in ourselves, more inner conflict and division can occur. This tension can come from how we got there, from the destination not being what we expected, or from our personal needs not being met. The stabilizing side of growth allows us to focus on what's here right now and supports expansion that comes from unfolding what's at our core, specific and unique to us, our desires, and our needs.

Like nature, we have seasons for different reasons, and like trees, we have seasons for expansion and others for stability. Each has its own purpose and duration. After that moment under the tree, I continued the projects and work I needed to, but I put a pin in pursuing anything new. I went inward, to reflect and rediscover myself, to find the footing and sense of self I had allowed to drift. I'm sharing in these pages what supported me in those months. The important switch for me here was that I didn't use that time or these practices to try to change or fix who I was in this world. I let it be okay to be right where I was and let that be enough.

When it came to making daily decisions, I held on to the phrase, "If it isn't a heck yes, it's a heck no," regardless of the logic. I still fall back on this idea to remind myself of my agency when I need to. I let my instincts guide me as I regrouped, reordered, and reconsidered how to move forward. I started taking care of myself, pared back my output, and focused on what I could give quality attention and time to, rather than just crossing things off my list. Sometimes this meant I would turn down coffee meetings with acquaintances to schedule extra time with my closest friends.

I think of this rearranging of my life and my work as working on puzzles. There are different pieces for different areas of my life, and I had to turn over each one to see where and how they might fit together. Unlike with real puzzles, we can put the pieces together to create whatever picture or design we prefer. The hard part is knowing what and how we want it to look using the pieces we currently have. It's up to us to be honest with ourselves, sort through our puzzle pieces and place them in a way that works best for us.

When we start evaluating and reflecting on where we are, we might default to comparing ourselves to others. Or you may have a specific set of life milestones you hoped to achieve by a certain age. Like anyone else, I sometimes worry about my age and whether I might be running out of time to have kids or buy a house. It's understandable when we face societal pressures and see family or friends seemingly achieving all we want to, but life isn't a linear path; it's a vast, ever-evolving landscape. When we can anchor in the idea that we are all on our own timeframes, we can better recognize that our existence in this life is not straightforward and that there is no hierarchy. Today, we are here, and everyone is in a different place and stage.

Looking at a tree, we see it simply where it is, a singular location, evolving in its own time; there is no tree ahead of or behind another. Like them, I don't believe anyone is ahead or behind; they are right where they need to be at this moment. Trees grow from their center into the type of tree they are, without measuring or comparing to anything else. We all grow at different speeds and in different ways. That's how it's supposed to be. There is no catching up to do. If we all did it the same way, life would be boring, and there would be no way to discover new things. We wouldn't be honoring our true needs and desires. To look more closely at where we are as individuals in the present moment, we can draw on the weather, the seasons, and our responses to them to reflect on ourselves and our circumstances.

Building stability to withstand weather, change, or growth isn't typically seen or perceived as progress on paper; it's felt and experienced. We often want to rush through to get back to expansion, but stability can require pauses, reorganization, and reflection instead of pushing forward. Focusing on stability may look like declining new clients, saving money for a future project, or working more behind the scenes. It can feel like you're not moving, when in reality, you are creating the atmosphere that allows you to move more sustainably as you regain your footing and clarity. It doesn't always look like progress, but it shapes how you experience it and what comes next. Even when it feels like stagnation, it's about strengthening and trusting the season we are in.

Being in a transition or "dormant" season can make us feel lost, but there is a time for everything. A tree doesn't hang on to its leaves in the fall out of concern for how long winter might be. New leaves return in their own time. In the same way, a tree doesn't drop all its leaves at once to bring spring or new buds sooner. A season of rest and retreating inward is part of what allows new and healthy leaves to return in spring. It releases them gradually, in their own time. If we honored our own seasons a bit more, what might we notice about the one we are in? Being honest with yourself about what you need and meeting those needs is the foundation of sustainable growth that balances expansion with self-stability amid life's changes. And while we may feel pressure from others, society, or even some part of ourselves, in this moment, there is nowhere we need to be but here.

Strengthening and building stability isn't just for our own expansion; it's also so we can better brave whatever weather may come. The weather is like life's circumstances and the changes that happen outside of ourselves. We can't change the weather, but we can adapt and respond to it as needed, which helps us navigate it. Weather and change are natural, but they can throw us for a loop or challenge us in ways we don't expect. When things happen, it doesn't mean we are doing something wrong or that we won't feel secure again. The sun will always reappear eventually, but when a storm hits, it's our basic needs that can make or break how we weather them.

If a plant isn't looking well or isn't growing, we look at its environment and see whether its basic needs are met. Others have suggested we can take the same approach with ourselves by looking at what might be contributing to how we feel instead of assuming something is wrong with us. You may have picked up this book because you're tired of the pressure, external or internal, to improve yourself. It's important to notice where we are and whether we are taking care of what's needed right now before trying to reach a new level. When we don't look or feel the way we think we should, our default might be to blame or target ourselves for the changes or growth we need. Yes, we have a responsibility and different ways we might respond to our circumstances, but that doesn't always mean we have to act or push or *do* more.

If we feel overwhelmed by our lives or are pushing to reach new heights, we might focus only on actions we hope will bring us to the other side sooner, putting off the time we need to tend to our foundational needs. For example, I have a tendency to shift my focus to whatever comes up in the moment, like responding to a new email right away or answering a call in the middle of something I had already planned to do, like work I had set aside time for or even taking care of myself, instead of sticking with what I had already decided mattered that day. I tell myself that if I take care of it now, I won't have to think about it later. But there is always something else coming in, and in the process, I end up putting off my own needs and the things I had intended to prioritize. This means I have to actively choose myself and my relationship with my inner experience. Sometimes that looks like taking a deep breath before answering the phone or responding to something new and asking myself if this is a good time to answer it, or staying with what I'm already doing instead of immediately shifting my attention. It can also look like stepping away, even briefly, to check in with myself.

Expansion, stability, and overall growth look different for everyone. I'm not suggesting we should perfect our self-care routines or that we have hours a day to devote to ourselves. That's not practical for most people, myself included. But are we maintaining our basic needs? For me, that means spending time in nature, moving my body, and staying hydrated. It's also about eating a balanced diet and, in a practical sense, keeping to my set budget, getting enough sleep, and getting ready and dressed for the day, even if I have nowhere to go. These are small, everyday ways I take care of myself, and they have a direct impact on how I feel and how I show up in my life. They don't always feel like an accomplishment, and they may not look like much from the outside, but they support me in staying aware of what's happening in and around me.

For many of us, we may already be doing some version of this, or we may know what we need, but it can be hard to maintain when something new enters our lives or when things feel uncertain. Our relationship to ourselves, our lives, and our circumstances is always in motion, so it's important to check in with ourselves and honestly ask, "Am I taking care of myself and what I need right now?" That might look like noticing you haven't moved your body in a few days, that you're more tired than usual, or that you've been pushing through without a break. It might be as simple as drinking water, stepping outside, resting, or returning to something you know helps you feel more like yourself. If you realize your basic needs are not being tended to, returning to them is always the first step toward lasting growth and a steadier relationship with change. If you are at a time in your life when all you have the energy for is your own version of the basics, know that is enough. The point is to look at our self-stability amid expansion and growth, and at our relationship to ourselves and to what we might learn. To be self-stable, we have to know ourselves and be able to meet ourselves where we are. That also asks us to recognize when we need support.

Healthy forests are made up of healthy trees, but expansion isn't always our decision. Sometimes change can force and require us to adapt and grow in ways we didn't plan. Growth and a balanced approach to change require health. When we are healthy, we can be ourselves more easily. Health and inner stability mean not only being strong but also being flexible so we can respond to circumstances with confidence and ease. To have a balanced response to change, we need to be honest about what we truly need. Inner stability starts with our relationship with ourselves, but we don't have to do it alone. We can explore and engage in self-discovery while connecting with others for help.

Being more of who we are requires us to recognize where we are, what season we're in, and what we need. We can't rush our seasons and expect sustainable growth. Growth and being all that we are require rest, reflection, and time. If we never give space for the seasons that look like a pause, we won't be able to fully turn our learning into wisdom. We have to choose ourselves—nurturing our growth through reflection and connection with our present state, building stability so that growth comes from our center. Bettering our connection to self allows for more self-compassion, greater patience, and a deeper understanding of ourselves and the world around us. To find stability and maintain sustainable growth, we don't have to alter who we are; we become more of who we already are.

REFLECTIONS:

- What season do you feel like you're in as a whole? One of expansion or more about stabilizing? If your current circumstances or life were represented in one of nature's seasons (spring, summer, fall, winter), which one would it be and why? Are you in different seasons in different areas of your life?

- What would you say the "weather" of your life looks like right now? Sunny? Windy and rainy? How are you feeling within it?

- How would you describe the environment of each area of your life? How do they feel?

- What does balance look like to you? How might you maintain or support more balance in your life?

- What basic needs do you have that help you feel stable and able to handle the weather or changes as they come? Are they being met in your daily life? If not, what adjustments could you make, or what help could you ask for, to better support yourself?

- What are you learning about yourself, the season you're in, and the weather you're experiencing? How does your relationship with yourself feel currently? What does it look like?

PRACTICES:

- Pieces: Take one area of your life and reflect on each element of it like it's a puzzle.

  - What "picture" are you working to build or create? Where are you in the process? How does each piece or element feel?

  - What pieces are fitting together well? Which ones point toward a different picture or outcome? Are there pieces not fitting together as well as you thought they would?

  - What actions or changes might you make to see the picture more clearly?

- You might find it helpful to draw a diagram and rate how each element feels, journal what comes up, or talk through your discoveries with someone you trust.

- You can return to this with other areas of your life as you feel called to.

• Celebrate one thing about the season you're in or something that feels meaningful to you right now. Share it with a couple of people close to you and let them celebrate with you.

3

Inner Core

To be you, you have to know who that is. Disconnection from my center has always been a gradual process; it snuck up on me. It would happen when I jumped from task to task, week to week, without a break. When I said yes when I really meant no. When I didn't move my body or nourish it the way I needed, and through many other small moments strung together where I chose something before checking in with myself.

Eventually, I would recognize how drained I felt, stretched thin and unbalanced. I'd find myself overworked, signed up for situations I didn't like or want to be in. My driving force was that if I was better at controlling my emotions, thoughts, and how my body felt, I would feel and do better. What I actually needed was to feel safe and secure in my body. I needed to know how I felt without relying on a reference point or another person, rather than looking outside of myself to decide how I was doing. If someone else was happy with me, I felt okay. If I received positive feedback, I was doing well; if I didn't, I wasn't. If the people around me were in a good mood, I could relax. I was depending on those cues to tell me how to feel, instead of knowing it for myself.

Looking back on my life when I felt off balance, there were days, weeks, months at a time when I was so over-scheduled and on autopilot. I couldn't tell you what was happening at all from my neck down. It was a constant cycle of something new to focus on: a job or position, a show, homework, a project to finish, more clients to secure. There was always something I was working on, and my default was to put myself on the back burner.

Early in my life, I always had something to act as a buffer between me and how I felt about what I was experiencing. I avoided myself like an awkward acquaintance. My need for a buffer was constant in my daily life, down to the simplest tasks like cleaning, homework, walking to class, or driving. I always needed music or something to keep me from my own thoughts; I couldn't just be with myself. I used books and entertainment to escape what I was experiencing.

My family had used TV and movies as a pacifier for conflict and emotion, and I continued the pattern, filling any "dead air" with something. To further circumvent any problems, I filled my head and time with constant ideas, input, and advice of others. Even between classes, if I wasn't with someone, I would call or text my mother to fill the time. I didn't like quiet or stillness; it made me uncomfortable and restless. I barely noticed my body or how I felt, and I struggled to connect with myself emotionally.

My self-disconnection left me feeling unsteady, weepy, and easily upset. If something popped up or changed my plans, I would adapt, but internally, it was a struggle. I felt beaten by the waves of what was happening around me, craving routine to keep me in control. I only knew how to absorb what was happening around me, and trying to hold it all was weighing me down. I was always on edge, rushing to take care of everything and everyone around me, leaving myself out of the equation without even realizing it. It was what I felt I should do, what I needed to do, but the sense of urgency smothered me.

The more time went by, the more my instincts and connection to what I wanted and how I felt dulled. I thought I was getting better at going with the flow, but I was actually becoming numb to myself. Part of that was because I believed that slowing down to find my footing would mean changing my plans or falling behind. I felt the need to ignore any unwanted feelings, in fear they might tell me something I didn't want to hear or hold me back from where I wanted to go and what I wanted to do.

Slowly, I began reconnecting with my core self, who had always been there, and as I did, I began to unfold more. It started small, with simply being with myself so I could remember what "me" felt like again. Having a relationship with who you are isn't about reinventing yourself; it's about meeting more of who you are. Choosing you isn't about choosing a new you; it's about choosing to connect to the you that's already here, just like the core of a tree. Trees grow new rings around their core each year, but the core remains the same. Who we are also remains, but what we experience, the stories we carry, the beliefs we hold, and our environments can lead us to feel out of touch with ourselves.

If we don't spend time with our true selves, how can we know ourselves, and if we don't know ourselves, how can we be ourselves? Choosing you means having an intentional relationship with yourself, seeing what's happening from the inside out, not just how things appear from the outside. This isn't about spending an exorbitant amount of time alone on top of your already busy life. We don't have to push others out, ignore them, or burn any bridges to connect with ourselves each day. Just like any relationship, it's not necessarily about the amount of time you spend all at once. Sure, any time or way we can connect with ourselves can benefit us, but at the end of the day, it's about the consistency of our interactions and how we show up within them. Small, consistent moments of connection can build over time in a way that the occasional longer stretches don't. You might already do this in your own way. Maybe for you, this looks like meditating, quiet mornings with a hot cup of coffee, or simply a few deep breaths before getting out of your car at the end of the day.

Choosing you means taking time to be with you and noticing what "you" feels like. Think of when we have a friend over for a visit, and they leave, but for a little while afterward, we can still feel their presence, their imprint in the space. We may recognize it more internally: after getting off the phone with a loved one, we can feel a warm, light-like sensation in our chests. We can feel and connect to our own presence in the same way. For some, connecting with your core self may feel more like remembering. When I connect with how I feel, in essence, it feels a lot like how I felt as a kid playing make-believe in costumes, where anything felt possible, or how at ease and excited I felt celebrating on my wedding day.

I find myself overly reliant on my eyes, perhaps more so because my eyesight isn't great. Thankfully, we live in modern times with corrective lenses; otherwise, in a different time period, you might find me begging on the street or working as a scribe, my face pressed against some parchment, smeared with ink. Since I depend heavily on my glasses, I feel extremely vulnerable without them and tend to rush to get them back.

One time, the arm of my glasses broke, and I had to hold them up like opera glasses. I had to wait a week for the new pair to arrive. Keeping them on while using both hands wasn't practical, so I found myself having to stay in that vulnerable state longer than I would have liked.

That experience showed me something: I didn't know how to feel safe in open, undefined space, literally or figuratively. My eyesight gave me a sense of control over my environment, but without it, I had to surrender that feeling of control and rely on other senses to remain calm. In taking my glasses off, I became more hyperaware of other sensations. Closing my eyes has the same effect. Now, intentionally spending time with my eyes closed is the simplest way for me to connect with my inner core.

While disconnection can happen slowly over time, the reconnection to self can be almost immediate, but it's not always comfortable at first. The idea of spending time in stillness or quiet with or without your eyes shut can feel really uncomfortable. There can be a tension of boredom or the push to be productive. Thoughts and ideas might be racing, or you may begin to feel anxious or a need to rush back to reality. That's normal, especially at first, but you don't have to change it; you can simply notice it.

The idea is to cultivate a few minutes of free, open-ended space and connection to you, no matter how you may feel or how things may look at that moment. It's a chance to wonder and pause, not a time to fix, plan, or sort through it all. It's an opportunity to simply be, acknowledge yourself, and reconnect with your sense of self and how that feels. For many of us, closing our eyes not only forces us to stop, or at least slow down, physically, but also creates a stillness and space within. In this space, we can better sense our own presence.

Physically closing our eyes can help us sense what is happening in ways our eyes can't. When we are uncertain, it's easy to rely on how our situation "looks" from the outside, leaving us unable to gauge how we feel *inside*. Closing our eyes can help us practice *being* where we are for however long we need or want.

What I had to learn was that taking time to be with yourself and reflect isn't about stopping progress. It's not about losing or wasting time; it's about gaining perspective. In choosing to connect, we can better learn and understand our wants and desires, what feels good to us, and what doesn't. There is no one way this should or has to look. When there isn't an expectation of an outcome or judgment, it's easier to allow what's here to be here.

When I practice this, it looks a little different each time, yet it remains simple. I take a few moments to be alone. I get comfortable; I close my eyes and just breathe and *be*. Some days, I like to sway or move while I'm here. Sometimes I use my hands to connect with my body, track sensations, or rest them somewhere that feels supportive, like one hand on my abdomen and the other on my chest. This helps me focus on the moment and explore the sensations I notice and where they show up in my body. I don't focus on trying to clear my mind or breathing a particular way; I just show up and see what's here today. The most important thing to me is that I don't try to change or create anything out of what I feel. Some days, feelings and thoughts come up, and I let them join me, but what I'm connecting to and focusing on is my center and who I am beneath the emotions and thoughts that emerge.

I do this at least once a day, but more commonly in the morning and evening. It can be really supportive, yet simple enough to do whenever you need. Whatever way you choose to try, if you do, it should feel good to you. If this idea of connecting to your inner core is brand new to you or you would like a structure to follow, you can try this:

1. Get somewhere alone for the next few minutes. You can sit, stand, lie in bed, whatever feels right for you in this moment.

2. Give yourself some silence or put on some calming music if you would like.

3. Get comfortable and close your eyes. To stay more focused, I try to keep them in place while closed.

4. Take a few deep breaths. In through your nose, out through

your mouth. Smooth and slow. Try to make each one slower than the one before.

5. Put your hands on your body. One could be on your heart,
   one on your belly, or on your lap, whatever feels comfortable.

6. Begin focusing on your core, directing your attention to
   the center of your body. You may consider "dropping
   in"—sinking your attention into your center. Connect to
   how your core self feels, not how the day felt, but how you
   and your body feel. The sensations, the essence of you.

7. Feel, sense, and notice how "you" feel. For me, my center
   feels expansive, alive, and bubbling. With my eyes shut,
   the sensations I feel evoke an image of shimmering pink
   light. No matter what I'm going through, when I connect to it, it never feels heavy or contracted. Your core
   self will feel and resonate differently from mine. For you,
   it may feel like a physical sensation, a texture, a shape, a
   color—or maybe envisioning an actual tree core works for
   you. There's nothing you need to do other than breathe
   and allow whatever it may feel like for you to be what it is.
   You don't need to control or change it; you only need to
   notice it. Spend a few breaths or minutes here.

Like a tree standing right where it is, just being here for these few
moments is enough. In doing so, we give ourselves a chance to be

who and where we are right now, without having to change what we might find.

In the hustle and bustle of life, it's not about the time spent; choosing you is about consistency. It's in the little moments, brief check-ins, seeing how you are without trying to change anything. What if this is exactly where you need to be right now? What if it's okay and safe to simply be here? Acceptance of what the present you and moment look like doesn't mean you are choosing to stay the same. In practicing this regularly, we may become more familiar with our presence, not just with our emotions and thoughts. When I started intentionally spending a few minutes with my eyes closed each day, I noticed that my presence felt the same and, in time, my awareness of it and how much I could feel it strengthened. By connecting to who we are beneath our stories, beliefs, and what we're experiencing right now, we can feel more relief, permission, curiosity, and steadiness, and have more energy to do what we need and want. When I'm connected to who I am, and have always been, there's a sense of ease that can happen internally.

By just observing, I became more aware in my day-to-day life when things came up for me to look at internally. Because of the connection I was building to myself, creating more space and opportunity for awareness and honesty, my sense of safety and inner security improved. Sitting with my own presence didn't change who I was or my circumstances. It gave me a chance to see myself more clearly and helped me be more myself when I opened my eyes again.

I want to be clear that connecting to our natural presence isn't about bypassing or ignoring feelings that appear. We are just momentarily connecting to who we are underneath, either before or after looking at those emotions. If emotions are already present and coming up, I find it best to feel and work through them first, then find my center again. I will share a way I start to process my emotions in a later chapter.

Our inner core, who we are at our deepest level beyond our past, feelings, and actions, is unchanging. At times, we can become detached from ourselves and our center without realizing it at first. If we cultivate time with ourselves and pay attention to how we feel, we begin to notice which actions and choices bring us closer to who we are or move us further away from our core. When we know ourselves at that deeper level, we unfold from the foundation of who we are.

REFLECTIONS:

- What is your connection with yourself like when things feel uncertain or busy?

- Have you tried sitting with or connecting with your

essence? What helps you connect with yours?

- What does your presence or essence feel like at your core? What do you notice about it? Does yours feel or look like a light, too? Does it have a color? A texture? A shape? Another sensation?

- What do you notice or feel after connecting to your presence?

- How might you connect with or remember your center throughout your day or week, if you don't already?

PRACTICES:

You can explore any of the reflections above through these practices or simply try it on its own.

- Spend a few minutes with your eyes closed to connect to your core self, what "you" feel like (use the steps in this chapter if needed). Try it once a day and notice how you feel after a week. What are you observing about yourself?

- Once you've connected with your center, you can experiment with saying the word "yes" a few times, either aloud or in your head, and see how it feels in your body. It may feel the same as your core self's essence, or like the volume is turned up, or an entirely new sensation may occur, like warmth in your chest.

- You can then try this with the word "no." When I do this, it's an immediate contraction and an odd feeling in my chest; it doesn't feel as good as my baseline. You may not notice any difference, and that is okay, but it's something you can play with and explore. Knowing what a yes feels like in your body—and what a no feels like—may help you make decisions with greater confidence.

- Once you're comfortable with how your center feels and whether it feels safe and accessible to you, you may ask yourself: What is present within me today?

  - Notice what you feel in your body. Is there a tightness in your chest? An emotion coming to the surface? There's no need to label or understand what is happening right now; only feel and observe. Allow whatever is here to be here for a few moments. *Later in the book, there are options for what you might do when emotions come up, but for now, it's enough just to witness what you feel in your body.*

4
Roots to Crown

B eing who we are isn't just about connection to the deepest part of us. It's about embracing and connecting with all of who we are, being whole with ourselves. We can practice observing, embracing more of who we are, and expressing more of how we think and feel if we choose.

There are parts of us we may have tried to cut off, ignore, or hide for a variety of reasons. We may have worked to shrink or morph who we are into who we think we should be or are pressured to be. When we reflect on different parts of who we are, it's easy to assume or judge what their presence means about us. Because we don't have to change what we find about ourselves, we can look at those parts, what we think and feel about them, and how they relate to the rest of who we are. From there, we can learn from them.

I was nine years old when my then-youngest sibling took their first wobbly steps across our living room. My parents and my other sibling were all there to see. It was the first time I had ever witnessed a child take their first steps on their own, and I was the proudest big sister. They were not an early walker, from what I can recall, but as a nine-year-old who had watched my sibling be born and even cut their umbilical cord, I was thrilled to see such a big milestone.

In my excitement, I cried out, cheering them on, giggling in delight, without a care. I was just a kid feeling joy. When you're having big feelings of excitement, it's fairly common for your voice level to increase, especially when you are young. Unfortunately, the part of this memory I remember most is not my sibling learning a new skill, but my parents abruptly telling me to be quiet. That moment was the first of many that rooted my hyper self-awareness and led to my self-monitoring, or rather, self-editing.

I'm uncertain if my parents had another reason to quiet me down, but even if they did, little me felt confused and put down for expressing a positive emotion. By that age, their dismissal of my less-than-pleasant emotions was already a part of our dynamic. Even then, I was a big feeler, and tears were my norm. My heavier emotions were not allowed in the presence of others; I was sent to isolated corners or my room to get over and move on without them. But this was the first time I remember having positive emotions shut down. It was one of the first signals I received that I was "too much."

As I got older and had more responsibilities, I was always met with a list of things to do to improve myself, the house, or help others before anything else. I stayed out of trouble, had good grades, and did everything I could to get things right. To the world, I was a perfect kid, but to my parents, there was always something I could do better.

What I experienced led me to confuse criticism as a prerequisite for connection.

If I eagerly shared something about my day, my father would either interrupt or wait silently until I was done, then simply ask, "Is your room clean?" or "How's your room looking?" That was it. If it wasn't up to standards, he would either get upset or ask what my plan was to clean it. If he knew it was already clean, he would respond to whatever I said with "cool," and an absentminded smile. There was rarely any further dialogue about what I had to say either way.

So I began to treat myself the same way, looking first at the list of things to fix before connecting with who I was. I spent many years worried about how I would be perceived because of the encouragement and pressure to self-edit, believing that if I didn't, I would be punished or rejected. This fear of being turned away by those I loved became a fear of being seen as I am. I was scared to be vulnerable and share what I enjoyed openly.

If I maintained who I thought I was, built on the identity of worrying about others' opinions, what were my actual thoughts and feelings about things? It made me wonder: are we denying parts of ourselves so other people don't, or simply glorifying things because others do?

Through the years, I heard a lot about how I was too emotional, fat, or serious. How I asked too many questions, cried too much, talked back too much, and cared too much. I needed to be more pure, more perfect. I was told I needed to smile more, grow up faster, be nicer, easier, be less, so I did to the best of my ability. I turned to perfectionism and anticipated how every one of my actions might influence emotions and the environments around me. If I were good, if I did enough chores, if I kept my room clean, if I dressed a certain way, if I stood up straight, if I didn't ask for help, then they would not only be happier in general, but they would also love and accept me more. My self-hatred was fueled by anxiety about causing a scene, drawing unwanted attention, and inviting judgment from others.

Because I was repeatedly told I was broken, sinful, or a nuisance to those around me, all I wanted to do was fix what I was told was wrong with me. I focused, as best I could, on eliminating and suppressing the quirks and traits that I or others didn't prefer. I tried to be more lovable, more likeable, to be who others around me expected me to be. I fought to prove myself to others instead of believing in myself and what I knew to be true. If I stripped parts of myself away, I could become someone else, someone people wanted. My self-editing led to dishonesty, mistrust, and questions of my self-worth. I looked outward and tried to keep my shortcomings from showing, while calling out, shaming, and cutting parts of my-self before others could. Eventually, I didn't know what to believe about myself or how to truly embrace how I felt and thought.

I hid things and parts of me that brought me joy, worried about how I might be perceived by others. Some things I pushed away on purpose, while other parts slowly faded because I stopped letting them exist. I remember once, around age 12, seeing a pink dress. It was a deep pink, almost rose-colored, silky, and flowy. It was perfect, and I wanted it badly. But I didn't buy that dress. I didn't even try it on. Why? Because I didn't think I could "pull it off."

I've always loved the color pink, but I routinely denied myself anything in that color because I believed I wasn't pretty or girly enough to like pink. So I always picked either blue or purple. They weren't really what I wanted, but I was worried that others would assume I thought I was more attractive or feminine than I was, or that I wanted to be. I found myself holding back my opinions, my sense of humor, and even things that meant a lot to me, like how much I loved to sing, because I believed I had to be especially talented to sing for fun.

When it came to my personality, I was told I was mature and responsible. Because of that, I was a stickler for rules, but if I made mistakes, I felt the need to hide them or lie about them. Of course, I was young then, and this didn't play out the same way as an adult, but the impulse to hide and keep myself small persisted. I wasn't keeping myself from buying pink items anymore, but at most events or parties, I struggled to dress up or wear anything that might draw attention, like dresses or skirts. I still wanted to avoid appearing as though I was trying to look nice, in case I fell short of how I felt inside.

As an adult, keeping myself hidden became even more about hiding my feelings and my true opinions. There is a time and place to express ourselves, but I found myself holding back and staying silent to keep the peace in my relationships. In doing so, not only was I denying a part of me, but I was also denying a deeper connection and understanding from those I was shielding myself from. I'm not talking about relationships and spaces that are harmful to us, but ones that we actually want to feel connected and whole in.

I've spent time reconsidering what and how I have labeled traits and interests, whether they were conditioned or reflect how I truly feel about something. Now I share my ideas and my mind freely when the timing and space allow. I sing whenever I want. I allow myself to be seen and to be more of all of who I am with those around me and in the world. I've embraced more of my actual style, and I'm excited about it, buying only clothes I love.

If you are struggling to accept where you are or who you are, or to meet the parts of yourself that are here, it can be helpful to look at the labels you or others have put on you. Labels can help us see aspects of ourselves, but they can also cut us off or limit who we are. Labels aren't inherently bad, but depending on our perception of them, we may respond differently to the meaning we've assigned them.

We may focus only on what has been labeled as good, bad, or healthy, and still ignore parts of ourselves that are true to us or that need our attention. For example, you might fill your schedule with things that are considered productive or good, saying yes to opportunities and responsibilities, while quietly putting off the things you actually need or enjoy, like time alone or something that helps you feel like yourself. Over time, those parts of us get pushed aside, and we may begin to feel resentment toward the very things we once chose. Parts of us can start to fade away, suffer, or break down, and resentment can begin to take shape in their place if we let it.

We can learn by acknowledging and embracing the parts of ourselves we don't like and look for the reasons behind that perspective.

Difficulty accepting parts of ourselves we don't like may not always stem from a fear of being seen or from hiding interests we prefer and enjoy. It can also come from resisting things about ourselves and pretending they don't exist. Maybe you also believe you're too sensitive, or think you're too outspoken, too shy, too needy, too impatient, too disorganized, the list goes on. If we look at why we don't like something about ourselves, we may be able to understand something new or remember things about ourselves we have forgotten.

There is something to be said for learning to accept and connect with ourselves, but it can quickly turn into judgment. It can be challenging to acknowledge and fully embrace the good within us. If you struggle with self-judgment, consider how you would respond if a friend came to you wanting to share something about themselves or their honest opinions. Naturally, you would meet them with openness and compassion. You wouldn't jump into explaining and analyzing everything wrong or what could be improved. We can be so quick to identify what needs improvement in ourselves that we overlook what's present and needed right now, and then we wonder why we don't like, believe in, or trust ourselves.

We may have spent time in our lives or in our relationships proving something about ourselves, what is true for us, or our worth to others, but we don't have to do that with ourselves. How we meet ourselves matters. It can feel like a chore, or it can feel like meeting with a best friend. It's not the time to beat ourselves up, critique ourselves, or try to change anything. Instead, it's about being who and where we are right now.

When we can accept and reclaim all we are, no matter how we label it, we can learn so much more about ourselves. I have found the best way for me to continue learning about myself is to engage in different activities outside my regular routine. Think of it like spending time with a friend—what would you do together? It can be as simple as going for a walk on your favorite path or grabbing a coffee without using your phone to keep you company.

We can't fully understand ourselves or be all we are if we don't recognize the parts that make us who we are and acknowledge what we honestly think and feel. If we criticize or try to cut off parts of who we are, we miss opportunities to build a closer relationship with ourselves and understand what makes us who we are. Choosing you is about acknowledging, embracing, and owning all the parts of who you are so you can show up in the world with confidence.

REFLECTIONS:

- How do you see yourself? Which parts of you do you focus on the most? What makes them hard to accept? What might that show you about yourself?

- Are there parts, traits, or interests that you try to hide? If so, why? Could you explore sharing or expressing one of these this week?

- Are there aspects of you or labels that are hard for you to accept? Why, and what do they show you about yourself? Could you give these parts a little more acceptance, love, or compassion?

- What parts of yourself or what you enjoy might you want to explore again?

- How do you currently spend your time or connect with yourself? How often do you spend time doing activities for yourself alone or without outside input? What does self-connection look like for you?

PRACTICES:

- Have a solo date or catch-up session with yourself. Do an activity that you enjoy solo and without input from another source, like a phone or book. Some ideas:

- ○ Go for a drive by yourself without the radio.

- ○ Go to a museum.

- ○ Walk your favorite trail or path.

- ○ Get a coffee or tea and sit in the shop for a little while.

- ○ Eat a meal with unfamiliar instrumental music in the background or in silence.

- ○ Take a long bath in dim lighting and good soap.

- ○ Leave your phone in your bag or pocket when waiting for an appointment.

- Write out a list of things you're good at and positive traits about yourself. What three are you particularly proud of and why?

  - ○ Ask 3 of your friends and family to list 3 positive qualities or strengths about you and share them with you.

  - ○ Consider putting all of them up somewhere you can see them.

  - ○ Try to incorporate any 3 of these skills or traits this week in an area of your life you don't normally get to use or haven't yet.

- Do some time traveling: Think back to yourself at different ages. What were your favorite things? Like a food item, a movie, a color, a song, an article of clothing, etc. Can you purchase or enjoy one of those items again this week? How did reexperiencing or using some of these items feel? Did you notice anything about yourself?

5

Our Rings

Like a tree grows rings around its core each year, we, too, have experiences that give us stories of what happened through our lives. Our stories, the beliefs we build and hold as a result of what transpired in our lives, are reflections of what we absorbed, were taught, or adapted to survive or thrive; they are not who we are at our core. They shape us and how we show up in the world, but they are not all that we are.

There have been many events in my life, and at the time, I believed I understood why they happened and what they meant for me. Missed job opportunities, unreturned feelings, or the loss of a friendship. It's easy to walk away from these kinds of experiences and start questioning whether you're not good enough, or that something about you is the reason it didn't work out. Then, days, months, or years later, you might realize there was more to it, or a completely different meaning possible for you to examine and explore. Like discovering the job wouldn't have been a good fit, you met the love of your life later that year, and that friend didn't act much like a friend after all. But we don't have to wait for the circumstances to reveal themselves or change before we examine what our ideas around them mean for us. The meaning or the story of something doesn't always have to get locked in.

Near the end of 2020, my husband and I decided we wanted to start trying for a baby. Little did we know that decision would turn into a two-plus-year roller coaster of emotions. At first, we kept our strategy simple, but after a few months, we began making more of an effort. We tried every trick in the book—tracking apps, diet changes, acupuncture—and none of it worked. During all that time and even for a while after we stopped trying, I was dealing with negative emotions and ideas about what our lack of success in getting pregnant meant. I found myself thinking, "What if I'm not meant to be a mom?" "What if I never get to be a mom?" "Is there something wrong with me?" "As a woman, this is one thing I'm supposed to do easily, and I can't?"

I carried around the self-given label of "infertile" and "childless" for a long time. We kept it a secret from our families to avoid the pitiful looks during the holidays and the inevitable tiptoeing. Every pregnancy or birth announcement I came across felt like a personal dagger to my dreams of being a mom. I was filled with anger and hurt. I avoided any talk about it with those too close to me while over-sharing my struggle with strangers, as if saying it aloud might make it easier to carry. I believed that explaining the emotional scars of not being able to get pregnant would make me seem, or even become, at peace with it.

It's been five years since we began trying, and while we aren't actively trying at the moment, my feelings around my experience have shifted from desperation to peace about the hope of what may still come. It would have been easy to have had that experience and walk away, convinced we will never or should not pursue becoming parents. But those ideas and beliefs were filters I didn't want to view my life through. So I started wondering if there was another, easier, even simply more neutral way to look at it.

I've asked myself multiple times over the years, if I could go back to that time and give myself a kid, would I? And the answer was and is no every time. I look back at who I was when I first pursued parenthood, and I'm so glad I got more time instead. Time to know myself better, to heal, to grow, and to unfold more of who I am before I gain the title "mom." There was nothing wrong with where I was or who I was, but now I can see how different the journey would have been. I know becoming a parent will change me in ways I won't know until it happens, but because of the work I've already done, I'm starting with more resources, experience, and knowledge than I had before.

As I reflected on the beliefs that surfaced, I started to see them differently. Some were still factually true, but they no longer carried the same weight they once had. It's like the way a tree grows a new ring after a difficult year. The earlier rings remain. What happened doesn't disappear, but something new forms around it, adding perspective and new information that can change how we show up and move through the world.

In my processing of my experience, the facts remained; I was unable to get pregnant and have a child during those few years, but what did I want that to mean for me? It's possible I won't conceive, but it isn't set in stone. And if it happens in a different way, would choosing to parent a child rather than birthing one make me less of a mother? I don't think so. This doesn't mean I'm operating or moving through life wearing goggles of delusion, pretending things aren't what they are. I can face the facts of my situation, but they don't have to determine who I am as a person or what I hope for.

Of course, it would be amazing to share that I'm pregnant now or have a kid, but I'm not even sure when we might try again. I just know we haven't given up hope, and it's not a story that weighs me down anymore. I'm not on the other side and a mother now, but it's a dream I'm still open to and walking towards. I'm still here, right? So, there's still time, and how the story will end is yet to be seen. This is an example of choosing what your experiences mean to you and how you want them to exist within you. Our stories come with us, but we get to define what they tell us.

Today, I can confidently say, I trust I will be a mom in some form. I can't tell you when, how, or in what capacity, but I know this because it's what we want. I'm not anxiously trying to determine how to make it happen—I just know it will be. Whether my kids are biological or chosen, I know I'll be an even better mother and give them a better life than I could have back then.

It no longer hurts when someone else announces their pregnancy or when a family member or friend has a baby. It doesn't bring me aching pain; instead, I get excited and take in all the baby cuddles I can. I'm genuinely happy for other parents, and I'm not comparing myself or our situation to theirs. This shift didn't happen overnight; it unfolded and transformed in stages. It was a progression of layers, working through aspects of my experience, the feelings that came up, and the meanings I assigned to things.

Sometimes what we believe about ourselves, or our lives, shows up in the things we say. I've noticed it in phrases like *"I never..."* or *"I wish..."* or *"I can't... because..."* When something I say or think doesn't sit right with me, I sometimes pause and ask a few simple questions: "Why not?" and "What am I worried will happen?" Sitting with these questions has helped me notice what might be underneath the thought. Often, there is a specific outcome I'm bracing for, even if I haven't named it yet. When I explore it, I try to stay with the first, most immediate concern rather than letting my mind wander into every possible future problem. The goal isn't to imagine every worst-case scenario. It's simply to notice what I believe might happen.

For example, if my car starts making a strange noise, I might worry that it will break down. If I pause and ask myself what I would do if that happened, the answer is usually straightforward. I would pull over. I would call for help, and I would figure out the next step from there. Thinking it through this way often makes the situation feel less overwhelming. The possibility hasn't disappeared, but I know how I will respond if it does happen.

Sometimes it helps to do this exercise with another person. When I've done it with a friend or partner, one person asks the questions while the other answers. The person asking the questions helps keep the conversation focused, so it doesn't spiral into every possible what-if. It's easy to start exploring what we are worried about, and a broken-down car becomes "I can't get to work," then "I'll lose my job," then "I can't pay to fix my car"—a partner can help you stay with that first concern and talk through what responding to it might look like.

What I've noticed is that this kind of exploration can reveal the meanings or beliefs I might be carrying about a situation. When I slow down enough to notice what I'm worried might happen, and how I imagine responding to it, my attention returns to what is actually true in the present moment. It becomes less about the past or every possible future and more about what is here now. From that place, I can see what I'm currently carrying and decide how I want to unfold with it.

For a while, holding onto the idea that I wasn't meant to be a mother felt like it was safeguarding me from the disappointment of trying and not succeeding again. I have found that I hold on to stories, beliefs, and meanings in my life and about myself to protect myself. Protection becomes my default. It's only when I examine those stories that I can see whether they help or harm me and my growth.

We don't need to judge ourselves harshly for negative ideas that we may hold, but when I'm observing them in myself, I try to remember that multiple things can be true at once. I may not be a mother now, but that doesn't mean I won't be or that I'm not meant to be one. It's not about changing the story or the event that happened or downplaying the impact it had, but about thinking about how you want to carry the story with you.

If you and I planned to meet on a park bench, we would most likely take different routes and make different choices along the way. Maybe one of us grabbed coffee first, maybe one of us walked instead of drove, or one of us showed up early, and the other forgot their coat. Either way, we both made it, and now we are two people sitting on a bench together. Our methods and decisions to get here shaped our arrival and how it looked, but what happened before our meeting doesn't dictate how it will go. Of course, there are exceptions, but we could take this moment to reorient, focusing on what's here and seeing where we might go from here.

What's happened previously in our lives brought us to this moment, but I don't think we need to rely on the past as much as we do to see where we are and how we might want to move forward. I want to use the past as a reference point, but not as the lens through which I make my next decision.

In my own observations of the beliefs and stories I carry, I've noticed how many naturally change over time. The way I see myself, what I care about, who is in my life, and even my tastes have evolved. With things like our interests, it's easy to see how our views shift. With harder circumstances, it isn't always as simple—or even possible—to see things differently. At times, the most difficult part has been allowing my perspective to change on its own rather than holding tightly to one that was no longer helping me.

If you have an experience that has a set meaning for you, I'm not suggesting you should alter it. There's no need to do anything with what you notice. We also don't need to track down or trace every belief we carry; we can let them reveal themselves over time. Sometimes the simplest way I notice my beliefs is by asking myself whether I like what I'm thinking, feeling, or trying to say in a moment. If something doesn't sit well with me, I may pause with it and see what it might reveal about what I'm experiencing.

Sometimes even learning a new fact about something can reveal an aspect we hadn't noticed before. Our understanding widens slightly, and our view expands with it. But when we are observing our beliefs, we don't have to work to change them or force a new perspective. We already change our minds and views about things throughout our lives. Sometimes the meaning of an experience quietly shifts over time, unnoticed. And sometimes meaning never arrives in a way that feels clear or complete. Not every experience resolves into something that makes sense, and that is okay, too.

Exploring our thoughts around our experiences helps us know ourselves more deeply. Reflecting on our experiences isn't about changing what happened, but about noticing what they mean to us and how they've shaped the way we see ourselves. Being more of who we are includes the past that shaped us and the beliefs that formed along the way. Like the rings of a tree, those experiences remain part of our structure, marking the seasons we have lived through. But they are not the whole of the tree. Life continues to grow outward from where we stand now, and new rings are always forming as we keep living, learning, and becoming more of who we are.

REFLECTIONS:

- What have you learned or recognized about the stories that have shaped you? How do they feel? Do you like what they say about you?

- What did you learn from the stories you hold on to? How do they support you? Or is the lesson complete?

- What would it mean to shift focus from "what if?" or what we may assume about something to "what is true?"

- What would happen if you let go of what you think you know and let who you are in this moment lead? How would you move forward if you held only the facts of what happened, rather than the meaning you've given them?

PRACTICES:

- Consider a situation you have been avoiding or feel stuck

in, and ask yourself, "What am I worried will happen?"

- ○ Notice the first, most immediate concern, rather than letting your mind wander into every possible future problem.

- ○ Once you've named the concern, ask yourself, "What would I do if that happened?" Talk through what responding to it might look like and what your next step would be.

- ○ If it helps, you can do this exercise with another person. One person asks the questions while the other answers, and the person asking the questions helps keep the conversation focused so it doesn't spiral into every possible what-if.

- Roll it Back: Consider reflecting on an experience as if it were a movie on a screen, or as though you're watching another person in the scene rather than reliving it yourself. The goal is to observe, not re-experience it. Try thinking in big-picture terms: "What happened?" rather than "what happened to me?" What do you notice? Is the experience leading you to believe something about yourself? If so, what?

If we reflect on what we believe about ourselves and what we have experienced, we may find stories that carry strong or complex emotions. It's important to approach these reflections safely and to remember that we don't have to process them alone. Consider reaching out to a professional or trusted friend for heavy or complex experiences that may require extra support.

6
Understory

When we examine the aspects of ourselves that form us, feelings inevitably come up. Our emotions can indicate our beliefs and the stories we hold, often revealing what we believe about ourselves or a situation. Unfolding all of who we are means being able to feel our feelings, even the ones we don't necessarily want to feel, such as anger, grief, or discomfort. When we connect with and navigate our feelings, we make space for all of them to be part of us and deepen our relationship with ourselves.

My parents didn't know how to manage and process their own emotions, so when I had feelings, they had to be for a good reason to be acknowledged. My anxiety, fear, and tears were seen as a weakness, a lack of fortitude. Anger or hesitation were seen as defiance, reflecting who my parents were. If your emotions were shut down, overlooked, or diminished by others when you were young, it's hard to validate your feelings. The only emotions my parents consistently supported were none at all.

I wasn't taught how to express my feelings in healthy ways. When I suppressed them, the pressure built, and as a kid, I was scared they might somehow take over. I didn't understand that feeling emotions and acting on them are two different things. Feelings are valid, but our behaviors aren't always. I was afraid of what I might do if I let myself feel everything, but I mistook that fear for being afraid of the feelings themselves. If I got loud in any way—sobbing, raising my voice—I would get yelled at. Fearful of the repercussions, I suppressed them all I could. I often knew why I was upset, but I believed that meant I didn't need to feel it. If I understood what caused it, I thought I should be able to move past it without letting it take over. Despite doing all I could to keep unpleasant feelings under control, the more I tried to ignore them, the louder they grew and the more uncomfortable I felt.

For the longest time, whenever feelings came up, I "documented" them in some fashion. I talked or thought my way around them instead of letting myself feel them. I could tell you what I was feeling and probably why, just by talking it through. Or I would journal my heart out to try to mend the crack in my emotional state. But I was staying in my head. I wasn't actually letting myself feel what was coming up in my body.

Feelings are meant to be felt, moved through, and with, but I was trying to process them or work through them at a distance. Turns out, I wasn't able to think my way through my feelings; I had to engage with and move through them. By not letting myself feel my emotions, I couldn't understand what was actually happening within them. I ignored my unwanted feelings, afraid they might tell me something I didn't want to hear or hold me back from where I wanted to go and what I wanted to do. Processing feelings mentally can help us see other aspects of them, but it can also keep us removed from them. My shortfall wasn't that I was processing my feelings; it was that I wasn't listening to them.

For most of my 20s, I practiced and learned to better express my emotions and eventually to give them room to be felt. One of the most revealing and relieving lessons I started to learn within my marriage was that I don't have to prove or convince myself that my feelings are real or that they have a reason to come up. Once I learned how to give them a safe space, ways to be seen and felt, and permission to express themselves as fully as I could, their intensity softened. Instead of losing control, I gained more breathing room. My feelings, like someone I would communicate with, were heard. I was not a stranger to dealing with my emotions before starting this book, but I was shocked by the inner work I had to do to get it into your hands.

I have always had a reverence for writers and their dedication to their craft, but writing a book is no joke. I had no idea putting my thoughts to paper would be so intimidating. Until you start, you only have a small idea of what it will look like. And who calls the shots? You do. As if it wasn't hard enough, you have to decide what to write, then actually write it. It's daunting to face a blank page with a head and heart full of things to share. Often, I would have the pieces I wanted to communicate, but I would get stuck, unsure how to say what I wanted or how to fit the pieces together. It's just you alone with your thoughts, without knowing what will come of seeing it through.

In the process, my first struggle was maintaining honesty and genuineness while making myself more visible. I've never been good at lying or speaking particularly highly of myself. So when it came to writing honestly about messy, unfinished parts of my life, you might think it wouldn't have been much of a stretch. The fact is, deciding to be fully myself on the page, leaving myself open and vulnerable to others, is one of the most terrifying things I've ever done. My goal was and is to help people, not publish a vanity project, but I'm told I still have to talk about myself, and I held back doing so as long as I could. It wasn't that I wanted to pretend in any way, but that talking about myself and my thoughts like this leaves me exposed to potential consequences and brings up fears I didn't even realize I had.

Fears of:

Not knowing what to say, how to explain myself, or whether the words would ever come.

That the words would come and I would actually publish them.

It not being good enough.

What my family or closest friends would

think—would they dislike it or find it silly?

Being seen, having my name forever tied to something, exposed to anyone who might read it.

The book being embarrassing without my realizing it.

Receiving backlash, being misunderstood.

But mostly, the fear that it won't help anyone.

Over the course of the year of writing, the trepidation I had came with doubt, overwhelm, and procrastination. Even the idea of "writing a book" felt overwhelming and, at times, made me want to avoid it altogether, so I changed it to "working on a project" to keep going. I just kept showing up, facing the fear, feeling my feelings as they came. This process took me through many highs and lows. I rewrote this book about four times before I even sent it to my editor, scared of how it might be perceived, struggling to decide which route it should take, and worried I wouldn't get it right. But I stayed the course, tried again, wrote more, and now you're holding the result.

So what have I gained in pursuing and completing this "project"? The biggest thing I gained? The experience of doing the hardest thing I have ever done in my life. I became more comfortable with the uncomfortable. While writing this book was the most confronting thing I've ever done, it was also one of the most healing (second only to getting married). I developed a stronger tolerance for uncertainty so that it no longer had the power to derail me. Over time, as I challenged my resistance and braved my emotions, I became less reactive and steadier in my resolve. Now, no one asked me for this book, but, following a whim of curiosity, I built more trust in myself to handle whatever comes up without abandoning myself or my feelings. My connection to myself, who I am, and what I want to pursue deepened. All while having no guarantee that anyone beyond my friends will even read this book, and you know what? I'm perfectly okay with that. Not because of any of the fears listed above; truth be told, if I had let them sway me, I would never have even finished my first draft. No, because I've made peace with who I am and what I'm putting on these pages, knowing that neither this book nor I is perfect, there's always room to grow, and there is enough sunshine for everyone. At the end of the day, even if only one person takes away one thing from this "project" of mine and it helps them on their own journey, even in the smallest measure, then it was worth it all.

Looking back, I've realized that much of my discomfort came from trying to ignore or shove down what was coming up rather than facing it. This came up many times while writing this book. Sometimes, when I didn't know what to say or how to say it, I would avoid writing. The discomfort of not knowing the answer right away and then ignoring or pushing it away would build up, making me increasingly uneasy. I could see that the discomfort wasn't the feelings themselves, but my avoidance of them. When I actually showed up and wrote, navigating my thoughts and how to explain them wasn't as intimidating as I initially thought. Of course, it was still challenging, but it felt more like working through a puzzle than something to dread. I feared the potential discomfort of feeling my emotions so much that the avoidance itself created a different form of discomfort. We can't get rid of or destroy feelings, so what does it look like to be in a relationship with them instead of seeing them as a problem to solve? They're signaling for our attention, so what if we gave it to them?

Emotions can show us what we want and need that differs from what we are experiencing, showing us that something needs more attention before there is a resolution. I believe many of our emotions reflect aspects of our true selves. They aren't who we are, but they may help communicate something from the core of who we are. Something to be noticed, not to be shut down. For me, it helps to see my feelings as young children.

You may think of emotions as singular beings, or assign colors or sensations to them, and I think that can be really helpful for connecting with them. When it comes to my own feelings, I struggle to define them as one emotion or idea, so I use little kids, or sometimes younger versions of myself, to allow more nuance to what I'm feeling. Rarely do I feel only one emotion at a time. How we label an emotion matters too. Is anger always bad? Is the presence of grief a signal that something is terribly wrong? The feelings themselves don't mean something is negative or lacking in you.

Feelings aren't the problem, but like kids, they can require different approaches and care depending on the situation, the day, the level of upset, and the person experiencing them. Our feelings may not always be correct or follow straight logic, but they are true to some part of us.

Thinking of my feelings as kids helps me remember to be kind and patient, and that I'm the adult responsible for them. I'm the one who feels them, and they come from my own filters and perceptions of life. Regardless of what happens in my life or how others act, I am still the one who cares for my emotions. I want feelings to reveal themselves so I can see what they might have to say or show me.

Not every feeling needs healing, and we don't always have to "name" the emotion coming up. We don't need to go looking for feelings to connect with or try to understand their place. They will make their presence known on their own, and we can simply allow them to be felt and witnessed.

Over the years, I've experimented with different approaches to connecting with my feelings. Some came from exercises I explored with practitioners, others from books or resources I encountered along the way. Through that process, I began combining a few simple ideas into a practice I return to regularly. It changes a bit each time depending on what I need, but this is the basic process.

1. First, I find a quiet space or someone I feel safe with, like my partner, and I set a timer for five to ten minutes, but you can start with as little as three. When the timer is up, I know I can transition back to whatever I need to do to take care of myself, the situation, or my day. The timer helps create a container that feels safe for me to focus on what's happening internally, rather than on external things or on

what's running through my mind.

2. If you'd like, place your hands where you're feeling sensations, or rest one on your chest and the other on your
abdomen, then close your eyes.

3. Then let whatever emotions you feel, or that come up, be
felt in your body. My goal in these few minutes is not to
think about what I'm feeling, but to experience and feel the
emotions.

4. Next, spend a few moments noticing and observing what
you physically feel with these emotions, trying not to slow
or change your breathing just yet, staying focused on your
body for up to a minute or so. Resist the urge to analyze
or understand what's coming up for now. Don't try to
fix, shift, or change the sensations; just be with them. If
you don't notice anything physically, that's okay; just stay
connected with your body rather than in your head.

   a. Where sensations are felt varies from person to person
   and can change with circumstances. What it feels like
   will also vary. Physical sensations may feel heavy, sticky,
   or uncomfortable, including pressure, tension, heat, or
   constriction.

5. As you pay attention to the physical sensations and allow
space for your feelings, you may feel the need to release or
express what you're feeling. For me, if I haven't been crying

already, this is normally when tears come up, and instead of holding them back, I let them out as much as I need.

6. After your minute or so of observing how your body feels, you may want to spend a few moments releasing any remaining tension or supporting what you feel. This may be screaming into or hugging a pillow, punching a folded blanket, vocalizing or sighing, shaking, etc.

7. When you're ready, close your eyes if they aren't already, keeping them in a fixed position to help you stay focused on what you're experiencing. You may also want to place your hands back on your body where you feel comfortable.

8. Then I begin speaking aloud, even if it's just a whisper, to myself, my feelings, or my body—whatever resonates in that moment. I acknowledge verbally what I'm experiencing. It might sound like "It's okay to feel _______." Or "That (event) was overwhelming, but I'm here." It's a few statements to remind myself that I am seen and heard, and that my feelings are normal and valid. The important thing is that I'm not trying to fix, analyze, reason, or respond with action in this moment. The goal is to validate the feeling and why it's coming up. I stay here until the timer goes off.

9. After the timer goes off, I check in again noticing what I need or what I might want to do next depending on the situation. Do I need more time? Something comforting like fuzzy socks, tea, or my favorite movie? Do I need to

move my schedule around a bit for the day?

10. Then, aloud and in plain language, I tell myself what's happening, what the plan is, and how I will respond to the situation. It may sound silly or unnecessary, but it's supportive in helping me find my footing again and so I take positive action when I'm ready. It encourages me to keep perspective on what happened and what to expect moving forward.

On harder days or with more intense emotions, I sometimes repeat the process after a little while. Additionally, I will give myself more time to be upset, to be comforted, to rest, or to process in whatever way I need. I like taking the day off to watch calming movies or read my favorite book without rushing. The key here for me is to decide how long to sit with what I'm feeling, then, when that time is up, I make a plan and take a small step towards what I need. Often, once I acknowledge what I'm feeling and the story behind why, I can respond in a way that allows them to exist and keep me moving in the direction I want to go.

Navigating feelings is one area in which I think we all need support from time to time, if not consistently. I believe the best form of support for our feelings often comes from being with them alongside others we trust. Frequently, I lean on my partner, sharing what I'm feeling to give those emotions space. When I do this, it's not just about talking through them. As I communicate what I'm going through, if emotions come up, I let them be felt and expressed alongside my words, allowing them to move through me physically, not just verbally. During or after this, my partner and I will do something together, like going for a walk, making food, or working through a task side by side. Being with someone I trust while I feel what's coming up helps me stay present with it, instead of trying to move past it or make sense of it too quickly.

It's important to recognize we don't always feel steady enough to be with what's coming up; we know ourselves and our limits best. What ways might we support our connection to our feelings in a way that feels accessible and good? Maybe, to start or when dealing with specific emotions, it's helpful to have someone with you—not someone to lighten or change the mood or influence how things come through, but someone who can simply let you feel. So if something that comes up feels too big to feel alone, trust that instinct and find someone to come alongside you.

Finding and practicing ways to connect with our feelings can help us unfold more of who we are. Creating space to feel them is important for understanding ourselves and being in a relationship with ourselves. Feelings are an inevitable part of being human; they all have their place. While feelings aren't all of who we are, they often carry a story or something for us to observe and understand. When we allow ourselves to feel big, messy emotions, connect with and validate them, and navigate life with them, we bring them into our life experience. In doing so, we allow ourselves to show up more fully as we are, instead of pushing parts of ourselves and our needs away. The deeper the emotional connection we foster with ourselves, the greater the unfolding of who we are.

REFLECTIONS:

- How do you view your feelings or yourself when strong emotions come up?

- What does experiencing or processing your emotions look like for you? Maybe it's movement, breath, vocalization, or tears. Do you have multiple ways or different methods for different feelings?

- What would you tell your younger self if they visited you today? Consider a couple of different younger selves that may need a message from you.

  - Journal or write a letter to little you.

  - Consider printing out a picture or two of your younger self to connect with when you need.

- What emotions do you most often push away or avoid?

- When a "negative" emotion comes up—after you've felt or expressed what you need to—ask yourself:

  - What do I believe about myself or the situation that is causing this feeling?

  - Was there a need or concern underneath what I'm feeling? Or did it just need to be witnessed?

  - Consider looking back at the last chapter's reflections to explore further.

PRACTICES:

- Explore what meeting and connecting with your feelings as they come up looks like for you.

  - Consider letting out sounds (vocalizations, humming, singing, sighing, or other sounds) to express what you're feeling. What do specific emotions sound like?

  - Try moving (swaying, rocking, dancing, or any movement that feels natural) with what you're feeling. How do specific emotions move or feel in movement? What does it look like for you?

- ○ Use the reflection questions above if they are helpful for you after you have felt through your emotions.

- ○ After feeling and reflecting, you might consider other ways to support yourself. Do you need to walk around the block, do some patterned or deep breathing, journaling, or talk to someone?

*If emotions seem to resurface that you have worked through before, that is normal. Try seeing it as an invitation to look at what's coming up again and whether something new is there. There may be a deeper layer in the situation, or in how you relate to it. It doesn't mean you didn't take care of your feelings before, but maybe something has shifted. Sometimes, unrelated events can bring up similar emotions, but that doesn't mean you've stayed the same or missed something the first time; it may be that you've grown and can now see them in a new light.

- Practice sitting in stillness, not taking any action for a few minutes. You can set a timer for ten minutes to start or go as long as you feel able. Simply sit, breathe, and be present.

  - ○ You can let your mind wander or focus on something in front of you, but the idea is to pause any productive or consumption activity. So you may want or need to fidget, tap your fingers, or make some other small movements—and that's okay.

  - ○ If you are not used to this, you may notice different feelings, such as a sense of urgency or boredom. I encourage you to stick with it and allow whatever sensations or resistance may come up.

- What do you notice? What is your response to what is coming up? How do you feel? What do you think contributed to how you feel or what you experienced in the stillness?

- Explore ways to move your whole body creatively or instinctively. Consider things that are new to you or outside your normal routine. You could try dancing or yoga, or simply explore your connection to the floor and how your body moves through space. See how you feel. What do you notice about yourself and your body?

7

Widening Our Roots

Our understanding can deepen through experience. I've seen it in my life and in the people around me again and again. Something would make sense intellectually, but the truth of it didn't become real until I've felt or lived it myself. There's a difference between what I know mentally and what I know in my *bones*. When it comes to experiencing new things, we can lack a sense of safety. Logically, we know we are "okay," but if we are in new territory with little "proof" to ensure our safety, we don't necessarily *feel* secure.

Growth and change, and the newness they bring, can challenge our sense of stability and safety. They ask either for more of us, or something different than what we have experienced before. This puts our ability to maintain a sense of self and clarity about what we are going through at risk. A strong enough windstorm can knock down the largest, long-standing trees if they don't have wide enough roots to keep them anchored into the earth. In choosing ourselves, we build our own stability, enabling us to grow while maintaining steadiness and safety. Stability helps us weather changes and anchor into ourselves.

Experiencing the same things over and over again can give us the illusion of safety. Routine circumstances help us feel comfortable and in control because we can predict what will happen. This is like deepening our roots into the ground—helpful, but deep roots without new experiences can create rigidity. When a tree's roots become too rigid, even strong ones can snap under pressure. When what we've known is no longer an option, our foundation is tested, and we begin to see whether it can bend or break.

Strengthening our roots might mean we need more routine, rest, and time to readjust and stabilize. Sometimes we need to deepen our roots before continuing to broaden who we are. In these cases, it's helpful to focus on saying yes only to what truly feels good to us, rather than pushing ourselves to learn and experience more.

Trees grow wider root systems, not just deeper ones, to withstand storms. Widening our roots gives us more ground to play with, learn from, explore, and expand who we are. When we have more stability within ourselves, it becomes easier to extend our reach and shape how we show up in the world. It's not just about deep roots to brace for a storm; it's about widening our roots so we can remain secure while bending in the wind.

I struggled with anxiety for most of my life. If I wasn't thinking about what I was going to wear, how early I needed to leave, and what I would have for my next meal, I was already finding something else to worry about. If I were going downtown, I would have at least three backup parking plans if the garage was full. My life was consumed by analyzing and planning what I said, how I walked, how I stood, how close I stood to others or to a counter, on and on. Several factors contributed to this, but one was that I was conditioned to be hyperaware of how I was perceived. Even when I was young, I was always considering what my face was doing, how my laugh sounded, and whether I was showing my crooked teeth when smiling. For every small decision I had to make during my day, I thought about and rehearsed it, considering all the possibilities.

To give you an idea of how deep this ran, as a kid, I hated having the windows down in the car, even when it was hot outside. I would get so stressed because the wind would mess up my hair. I always carried a comb and a compact mirror with me to help keep myself looking as nice as possible. I remember one day, my dad was driving, and the windows were down. My hair was flying around, and I was holding my hands to my head, desperately trying to keep it in place even though we were only going home. It was a sunny day, and I could tell my dad was happy, enjoying the fresh air—if I asked to roll the windows up, I knew he wouldn't see a reason for it and tell me no.

A few days before, there was a TV commercial for a water-enhancement packet or something mundane like that, featuring a carefree woman riding in a convertible and the line, "sometimes you have to let the wind comb your hair." As I was sitting there trying not to freak out about my hair, I remembered how happy and at peace that woman seemed. I remembered that line and started repeating it to myself to ease my growing stress. I made it home and immediately ran upstairs to fix my hair in my bathroom mirror. I was only eight.

Change, newness, or any form of spontaneity had only ever brought me discomfort and stress. I sought comfort from things outside of myself—food, verbal validation, support from others—and as I've mentioned before, the numbing distraction of movies and books. I planned and prepared for every possibility because I couldn't find stability within myself and didn't have the tools or knowledge to navigate my circumstances. It's difficult to see the way through when you're in the middle of your own storm. I needed a way to give myself more perspective, or at least a different one, either inwardly or in what was happening around me.

I've always been drawn to art, theatre, singing, dancing—all the typical forms of creativity and self-expression. They help me slow down, process what's happening internally, express it outwardly, and ultimately give me a break from whatever has been weighing on me. Creative acts don't have to be witnessed by others for you to gain insight into yourself, how you feel, or what you're going through. There is also the opportunity for different things to reveal themselves when there is no expectation of others seeing what you've expressed.

While I love drawing, dancing, singing, painting, etc., that doesn't mean I'm especially talented at them. At the end of the day, they are really just for me. There's a difference between developing your craft and being creative for creativity's sake. What I mean by being creative is specifically about exploring without a specific outcome in mind. Open-ended creativity requires experimentation rather than perfection and helps us practice flexibility and adaptability. Sometimes, especially when creating or working on something new, things won't go as planned, and you have to figure out another way to accomplish what you want. This shows you how you work, where you excel, and where you might need more patience or flexibility.

We can use creativity to challenge what we think, what we assume has to happen, and how something can be done. More often than not, it's in these times of exploring and doing something creative, or approaching something creatively, that I find just enough space to gain clarity, generate new ideas, troubleshoot a problem, or simply return to my center.

The other side of the coin is the ability to gain perspective and understanding through external experiences. Sure, I may consider myself a creative person, and that may help, but creativity isn't just for the artists, poets, and musicians. To be creative, you don't have to produce something new, and tapping into and exercising creativity isn't about doing more. Creativity doesn't have to take a physical form to be exercised. It can be in how we think about or approach something. This isn't about doing more or spreading ourselves thin; it's doing things differently, with curiosity and fun wherever possible.

There's an invisible cost to growing up too quickly and being forced to act only responsibly; play gets demonized, dismissed as frivolous, unnecessary, and unrealistic. I was raised with the idea that achievements require hard, grueling work to be considered valuable and worthy of our time and efforts. As a result, I resisted the things that brought me joy, the things that felt light and freeing. It's only been in the last few years that I have learned to bring play and imagination back into my life and realized that they don't diminish accomplishments; they only make them easier.

One way I like to explore and include more play in my life is by connecting with a fictional character. Writing this book was one place this showed up. As I said before, it was hard to face my fears and choose to keep showing up for this "project." I've always loved *Little Women*, particularly Jo March. If you're not familiar, she was a bit of a black sheep in her family, and I suppose her community in a way too. She's outspoken, strong-willed, and self-assured, and she was a writer. I've always felt like an old soul or born in the wrong time period, and the little girl in me loves dresses and skirts. So on days where I lacked motivation or had been away from writing for a few days, and coming back to it felt harder than starting did, I would do what I thought Jo might do. I would put on a long skirt, throw on a scarf like a shawl, light a candlestick, put on classical or piano music, and sip tea or coffee as I wrote. I even bought fountain pens, which are now my preferred writing utensil. I may have looked silly letting her lead as an alter ego, but you know what? I would write, and I enjoyed it. Playing pretend made it fun, less like "work," and took some of the pressure off. Dressing and acting like Jo March didn't make the process easy, but it made me feel more at ease within it.

We don't have to wait for ourselves or our lives to change before bringing joy and fun back into the present moment. We can enjoy being who we are and where we are along the way. One of the best ways to let joy take the lead is to say yes to the things we love. Some of the best moments in my life were the times I didn't wait or say no to having fun or doing something that excited me.

The idea of bringing fun back into what we do isn't about avoiding or never facing challenges; it's about not letting the challenges define how we feel as we move through them. Following joy and curiosity doesn't mean we're ignoring what's happening; we're just not letting the circumstances control us. Playfulness in our adult lives helps us reconnect with who we are at our core. Having more fun doesn't fix or change things, but it brings us closer to who we want to be and how we want to feel.

A few summers ago, I was hanging out with my friend, Sloane, when she and her roommate, Brayden, decided to go float the river. The weather was perfect, and they were planning to meet up with another friend of ours, Morgan. Here's the thing: these three were not only people I thought highly of, but they were also all very attractive. They were fit, athletic, and outdoors all the time; two were even personal trainers, and they intimidated me back then.

When they invited me to join them, I immediately declined. Now, I love being in and around water; floating is one of my favorite things to do in the summer. So why did I say no? Because my legs were in desperate need of a shave, and they wanted to leave right then. I didn't have time to shave even one leg, given their condition. Yes, it was summer, but I hate shaving. Even in college, I would shave just above my ankles on dates, enough to look "perfect" where it could be seen. I don't like having hairy legs either, but my leg hair is very dark and hard to maintain, so I keep them hidden, even from me. Just like I couldn't stand my hair blowing in the wind as a kid, I still preferred to be as "perfect looking" as I could, or at least in a state of imperfection I felt comfortable with. There was no way I was going to let people see how hairy my legs were in the middle of July.

Sloane and Brayden challenged my excuses, so I came clean. I was embarrassed to admit it to Brayden, but I told them about my "Yeti situation," and their response caught me off guard. "So? We don't care at all." They were nonchalant about it, not dismissive, but confused about why that would be a hesitation for me. So I asked myself, why not? And besides my obvious anxiety, there wasn't actually any other reason to say no. So I said yes.

I had not thought all of it through, though. Unfortunately, we weren't just hopping in the car and getting into the water. We had to go to Morgan's uncle's house to fill the tubes. I would have loved to stay in the car to hide my Yeti legs, but the heat that day made it impossible. So there I stood in front of Morgan's uncle and male cousin I've never met before, with my unshaved legs. I was comfortable around Brayden, and women would get it, but two more men? I was trying not to flee in shame; it was agonizing internally, but nothing bad happened. Sloane was struggling to get her tube filled, Brayden was cracking jokes with the cousin, Morgan was chatting with her uncle, and no one cared or said a word. I was unshaven and safe.

And being on the water that afternoon was one of the greatest feelings I've ever had. I know that sounds dramatic or ridiculous, but it was the first, and to this day, one of the most liberating things I have experienced. Getting to do something I love while being fully and wildly myself in front of not just my friends, but other strangers on the water floating past us. I will never forget it.

I still prefer having my legs shaved in public, but the experience, or maybe more accurately the exposure, allowed me to see and consider other things about me and how I live my life. What else have I been saying no to? Are there standards I've set for myself that are holding me back? Are there other ways to do things I haven't considered or have but avoided because they were unfamiliar to me? Does the discomfort I'm feeling actually mean I'm in danger?

I think it's important to acknowledge that even in fun experiences, making space for more joy and ease can, ironically, feel extremely uncomfortable at first. Like traveling to a place we've never been, it can be both exciting and daunting at the same time. We can learn to recognize when fun and discomfort can coexist in a way that supports us, and when something is simply not for us. It's still a form of change, and it can make us feel just as vulnerable as the change we don't ask for. If we are exploring something new and it stops being fun, we can pause and check in with ourselves, reconnecting to what's happening internally and steadying ourselves before continuing. We don't have to push through assuming fun will greet us at the finish line—unless that's genuinely what we want.

That's why I think the easiest way to practice feeling more joy in our lives overall is to play in smaller, often silly ways. Play opens us up to possibilities in ways that feel safe and easy, without the pressure to achieve an outcome. When we focus on the experience itself, we become more open to what we might learn from it.

Experiencing new things through play and creative approaches to what is already present in our lives expands our understanding. For me, the goal isn't to achieve an outcome; it's to explore without expectation. Having new experiences doesn't require changing our current reality or having a specific end goal in order to benefit us. It challenges our expectations about what we know and, as a result, can help us find more security in ourselves and what we are capable of. New experiences offer feedback that deepens our understanding of ourselves. It's in the playful moments of silliness that I get to peek beyond the lines I have drawn myself and see what other possibilities may lie ahead.

REFLECTIONS:

- Right now in your life, do you think you might benefit more from widening your roots and gaining new experiences to learn from? Or strengthening your roots, leaning on routine, and focusing more on your connection to self?

- What is your relationship to creativity while in the midst of change or in response to it?

- How might you bring more play, lightness, or even a little messiness into your process of growth?

- How might you do something necessary in your daily life in a fun or new way? When you try it, what do you notice?

- What would letting curiosity or joy lead look like in your day-to-day life? What are some small things or moments that light you up that you might say yes to?

PRACTICES:

- Try mixing up your routine—once a week or across different areas of your life—to see how it goes. Ways to explore:

  - Drive a new route or using a different mode of transportation to work.

  - Use the opposite hand to complete activities like brushing your teeth.

  - Flip your schedule; what you would normally do in the morning, try accomplishing at night, and vice versa.

- Try adding some time for creativity or an activity that invites self-expression, such as baking, painting, rearranging your furniture, or taking pictures.

- You can also create something, either letting it be "bad" or purposely making it bad.

- Choose a fictional character to embody in some way.

  - What was it like? What did you notice or learn? What did it show you about yourself and how you approach things?

- Say yes to the next opportunity that sounds fun or interesting. Of course, we should all know our limits and what feels safe, but if there's something we want to do, does it hurt to ask, "Why not?" a few times?

- Practice receiving the next thing offered to you without hesitation or resistance. For example, a compliment, having your drink paid for, an offer to help you carry something.

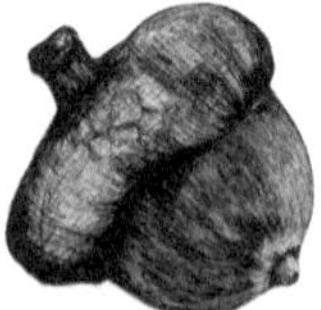

8
Room to Grow

When we feel secure in ourselves, we are better able to respond to change and what happens in our lives. Just like when we feel secure in our finances, we aren't fazed by an unexpected bill. When we observe and reflect on how we show up in our daily lives, how we feel and respond to life's unknowns, and what we have yet to experience, we can discover where we might need more perspective or space to lead ourselves better.

Neutrality creates space and perspective to learn and understand ourselves and where we are. Security in who we are, how we feel, and how we operate allows for greater neutrality, but neutrality is not devoid of emotion. For instance, even if we feel financially supported, we still enjoy getting money. When we can be ourselves and feel steady, we and our lives feel easier. As a result, we may find that we have the ability to respond rather than react. Neutrality helps us strengthen and stand where we are while we figure out or navigate our next steps.

In choosing to be who we are in the world, we will inevitably face resistance, both internal and external. When we're focused on taking action or on wanting to expand, unexpected obstacles or changes in plans will occur. It might look like our car breaking down or receiving negative feedback, and either over time or all at once, we may lose sight of where we are and what's possible. These moments can challenge our inner stability. Our vision, our sense of purpose, and our dreams can feel clouded when things don't go as planned, take longer than expected, or change direction.

If we are less neutral when something happens, we can learn from what's coming up. Internally, this conflict can show up as our feelings, which we've talked about meeting, but it can also look like procrastination, a lack of motivation, or pressing through blindly. I find that most people I meet are used to operating from a place of fear, guilt, or other feelings that may drive action but don't feel good. Externally, the resistance we experience may manifest as delays or obstacles in timing or funding. If we rush from deadline to deadline, ignoring the resistance or obstacles that come up, we can end up letting external factors determine our feelings and reactions.

Almost every job I have done has centered on using a computer. Especially when working from home, my computer is necessary to keep me going. Whenever I run into a technical issue, I naturally try to work around it or fix it as soon as possible. What I've noticed is that when I run into multiple disruptions in my work, I get increasingly stressed and push myself harder to make it through the current project. The urgency to meet a deadline, or my expectations for the day, creates pressure.

I can't tell you how many times I've been working on a project and hit an obstacle, then another, then another, and things feel clunky and are not flowing. In those moments, I would default to pushing through anyway because I just wanted to get it done so I could relax or move on to the next thing. Every time I did, I would end up having to redo it for some reason, whether I messed something up, misunderstood what I needed to do or how to use something, got new information that changed what I had already completed, found that it was no longer needed, or discovered an easier route. The fear, constraint, or guilt I put on myself to finish something only led to more work in the long run.

We don't always have a choice, but when we do, forcing output isn't the way. If I remain neutral toward issues as they turn up, I can feel more at peace with what is occurring and pay attention to what I can control. That doesn't mean we should let obstacles dictate how much or when we get things done, but when there are multiple issues over and over again, it's okay to slow down and get curious about what is going wrong or how we feel in the situation.

Is this program or tool the right one for my needs?

Have I eaten?

Do I need some water?

Is this an opportunity to take a break or switch to another task that feels easier?

Now, I use obstacles as a pause to reflect for a short bit before continuing. It's a check-in, not a "let's toss it out." When I run into technical issues, I don't have to assume that I'm behind schedule or get stressed. I can be neutral in my actions when issues come up. When things get delayed or don't go to plan, they often resolve on a different timeline and work out better.

I believe wholeheartedly that 99% of urgency is a made-up construct. Some people struggle with fear or with missing opportunities if they don't stay "on it" all the time, and they can exhaust themselves trying to maintain their output. A couple of years ago, I found myself feeling under immense pressure to meet specific work deadlines. Maybe it was the delirium of exhaustion, but I remember sitting at my desk staring at the birds in a tree outside. I was reminded that the deadlines and work I'm rushing to finish don't affect much outside these four walls. Yes, there were other pieces of my work that affected the whole, kept things moving, but in the larger scheme of things, the urgency I felt existed mostly in my own mind.

For instance, what happens if I get sick, and I'm unable to complete what's expected of me on time? Of course, this can add stress to the situation, but in many cases, nothing truly bad happens; we let people know, catch up when we can, or get help from others. The sense of urgency in a scenario may be driven by multiple factors, but most of the time, those factors are manufactured to some degree, too.

We carry this into other areas of our lives as well, with timelines we feel we're supposed to meet, like needing to have a certain career, relationship, or version of our life figured out by a certain age, or feeling like we're running out of time if we don't. Unless someone is in physical danger or something is being destroyed or harmed, there is little need for urgency or immediate reaction. Sure, quicker is often preferred, but it's rarely actually required.

I used to use my stress to push myself, rather than respond to what was happening in the moment. Our bodies often signal to us when they need a break, but when we get too zoomed in on deadlines or specific expectations and ignore our bodies, they can resist what we are working towards. I may experience brain fog or fatigue or overschedule myself to the point of getting ill. I used to operate separately from my body, but these signals are ways our bodies tell us to pause or that something should be adjusted. We may simply need to step outside for a few minutes, take a shower, or a nap. Taking breaks helps me when I feel blocked, and I get more done when I come back. Often, I find that the answer to what I was stuck on comes when I've stepped away and gotten some space from it.

We can be hard on ourselves in specific areas of our lives because of the expectations we set. In our efforts to improve ourselves or our lives as quickly as possible, we can end up adopting rigid plans and paths, leaving little room for exploration and play. Some of us, myself included, can take life too seriously. Of course, there are real struggles and problems, but I'm talking about the pressure, the nature or level of performance we impose on ourselves, so we can reach an intended outcome. I believe we are all doing the best we can, but if how we're managing the unexpected doesn't feel good or supportive, consider other ways to pause and reflect.

Our perspective of our experiences is often shaped by our expectations. In examining our expectations, we can learn to think and view our circumstances in a softer light. We can truly never know how something needs or is supposed to be. Even when we feel like we have clarity on that, it's not until after the experience has played out that we begin to understand how it worked or didn't, and even then, we are only seeing parts of it. We are limited to what we know about the present and can only observe how things work out afterwards. Too many or too specific expectations can limit what we see and understand, and how we feel in the process. When things don't go to plan, especially when it causes me some upset, I try to ask myself:

Am I really behind, or am I right where I need to be?

Is it messed up, or could it work out even better?

Is it wrong, or do I have a narrow or specific expectation?

It's not that we should never have goals or specific hopes, but there are multiple ways and paths we might take. Just because it's going differently than we planned or expected doesn't mean we are off track.

Sometimes we can struggle to be who we are where we are or be unsure of how to proceed. Instead of searching for energy or motivation, I look for what excites me about what I want to do. Wonder and excitement can propel us when we give ourselves room to explore them. There's one tool I use regularly to keep myself open to possibilities. It's my favorite because it creates more space internally and brings me back to myself and what I want. The practice grew out of exercises I did with a practitioner. Some of what I share here started as suggestions or small pieces of "homework" meant to help me notice how my thoughts and feelings shifted. Over time, I adapted those ideas into what I now call Walking Daydreams.

It's a simple concept, and you may already practice your own version of taking walks to clear your mind or spark ideas. Sometimes I choose a specific set of songs to encourage me, my steps falling into the rhythm of the music. Sometimes there's no music, no input, just my breath and heartbeat. Other times, I hum quietly to myself.

During these walks, I practice dreaming up my biggest dreams and my smallest hopes. I may whisper it under my breath or keep it inside, but I let myself imagine and explore: Wouldn't it be great...? It might be something small like "wouldn't it be great if I had all green lights on my drive home?" or "wouldn't be great if I got a free coffee tomorrow morning?"

I don't use these walks to plan or decide anything. The how doesn't matter, nor does it need to be possible at all. I'm asking myself what possibilities feel the most alive or interesting to me.

These daydreams get to be whatever I want them to be and as silly, unrealistic, or as heartfelt as I desire.

During my explorations, feelings of fear and uncertainty stayed behind. Internally, my Walking Daydreams feel like a full-body stretch with arms overhead first thing in the morning. They create this internal spaciousness and then fill me with more wonder and excitement without anything in me or my life having to change. I'm allowing myself to feel the expansion and excitement of my dreams and ideas before they are here. It's another way I get to practice connecting to myself.

At first, it felt sort of empty in a way; it wasn't this grand fanfare or a light switch turning on. It can feel silly to speak or whisper to yourself, but as the walks continued, I felt lighter and lighter. I began walking taller, with a different kind of energy in my steps. I would smile and feel joy and hope in what's to come.

What I've noticed in this practice is that the focus is not on "how." As a planner, I know how hard it can be not to start thinking about steps to make things happen, but the steps don't matter here. If there are obvious things you can do when you get home to point yourself in that direction, great, but it's not about willing the vision or next step into existence; it's about being open to options.

Walking Daydreams show us choice and potential opportunity; another way to check in with our core self and how we feel. They can help us get clear on what we want, so when choices pop up in our day-to-day lives, we can choose better based on the world and life we want. They make room within us for our expansion and unfolding, in all the ways that might unfold.

This practice can also be uniquely supportive when practiced with a partner or friend. When I practice it with my husband, we take turns building the daydream together, adding our own elements. We both beam brighter, and by the end, we feel closer and ready to continue where we are in our lives and goals. It helps by giving each other new ideas and ways we might accomplish something too. Many times, one person starts something, and the other expands the idea or opens it up.

Beyond these moments, resistance and obstacles we face as we go about our lives can give us an opportunity to check in and reflect on how we are responding and from what kind of place we are taking action. When we are aware of how we respond to things outside our control, we can meet life and its obstacles with greater openness, curiosity, and possibility. We can expand our vision by using feelings of wonder and hope to propel us. What the walks bring create more ease and neutrality along the way.

In those situations, they help restore perspective and emotional stability when life starts to feel too narrow. Over time, it has kept me open to new ideas and potentially easier routes. It helps me keep my center and my ability to dream for more and better opportunities. It gives me room to see or feel my immediate problems or expectations in a new way. They make me feel more at ease and excited about the future, rather than stressed or trapped by what I might be dealing with in the moment. They don't overlook or help me avoid my problems; they help keep me from being taken over by them.

As I spend more time choosing myself through practices like Walking Daydreams, the more I understand the choices I have in how I respond to my world. They help me gain perspective on myself and on what I want more of. The walks help me practice and embody how I want to feel and move in this world: expanded and whole. Broadening our vision, how we feel, and how we lead ourselves changes how we show up to the unknown.

REFLECTIONS:

- What would you do if time and money were no object? Is there something you would want to be known for by those around you? In five years, what would you like to say is true about you or your life? What do you want your day-to-day life to feel like?

  - Start small, or keep it broader if needed, like spending more time in nature or being more involved in the community. Write it down and practice letting yourself dream and long for something with hope, without needing to figure out how to do it.

- When a common obstacle or inner resistance comes up in your daily life, what is your default reaction?

- When you feel stressed or pressured to complete a task or achieve a goal, consider the expectations set by others, the project's outline, or your own. Are there any that are unnecessary or preferences rather than needs?

PRACTICES:

- Go on a Walking Daydream alone, with your partner, or with family. How did it feel? What kind of daydreams did you come up with? If you did it with someone, what was that like for both of you? Try one of these walks again in a few weeks and notice any differences.

- Create your own "Support Toolbox." When life feels heavy or we face challenges, it can help if we already know which tools or resources can help us reconnect to our center and find our footing again. You may have tried some different methods from this book while reading, or ones you found through your own experimentation. Note and continue to try different techniques as they spark your interest. What tools have you used that genuinely helped you? Which ones felt heavy or didn't fit for you? Which ones might you return to, and keep in your "toolbox?"

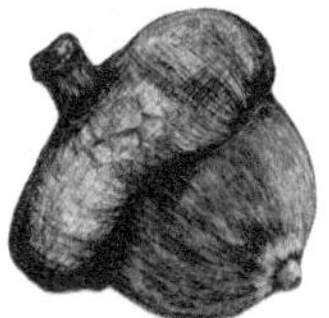

9

Extending our Branches

Choosing you is about coming back into relationship with yourself, your body, your feelings, and the stories of your past. It's focusing on our own growth rather than trying to force change. When we are stable and secure in who we are, we can expand in ways that feel good to us. Our expansion becomes an extension of our core selves—not above change but working with it and through it.

Sustainable and lasting growth occurs when our expansion is supported by our stability. We are still human in this world, so it's not about growing above things so we don't have to deal with them. It's about being more human, and who we are within the lives we are already living, feeling, and moving through.

When we cultivate inner stability, we are better able to bring joy and curiosity to how we show up and make an impact in the world. We can lean on joy and curiosity to extend our branches, connecting with and growing from our core selves and our true desires.

Expressing more of who we are outwardly means putting what we learn about ourselves into action through our choices and how we live our lives. What we accomplish can become an extension of who we already are and what is important to us. When we are fully ourselves, we are able to express more openly and honestly with those around us in ways that feel good to us. Life can feel full of possibilities when we know how to connect with our feelings and thoughts, and meet the day as it comes.

Your unfolding is yours. It doesn't have to be witnessed by many or by anyone at all if you don't prefer. Expressing ourselves doesn't have to be advertised or public; we can grow and expand quietly. This might look like creating more in our free time, volunteering more, or being more honest and open in conversations with others and in our close relationships.

When we choose to be in relationship with ourselves, rather than a product of our circumstances, we choose to be the leaders in our own unfolding. Being more of who we are allows us to use our individual strengths or the surplus of our internal resources to help others. When we are healthy, we are freed up and better able to support the people around us with our energy, interests, and skills.

Extending our branches is being more of who we are in the world and in our communities. Humans are meant to be in connection and relationship with others. Healthy trees make healthy forests. When we are rooted in who we are, our whole community benefits.

We can't outgrow cycles or prevent change, nor do we need to change in order to grow.

Staying present while living our lives can challenge us in ways we don't anticipate, and maintaining our relationship with who we are is a courageous practice.

No matter what season or change you might experience, I hope that you continue to choose yourself and your unfolding.

REFLECTIONS:

- What have you learned or remembered about yourself recently?

- What might "extending your branches" look like for you? How would it feel? How might you share your strengths or passions and help others?

- What might you choose or try next, knowing what you know about yourself now?

- How might you continue to be who you are in your community, your work, and your relationships?

- What you have done or discovered while reading this book?

- What can you celebrate about you, where you are, and where you're heading?

A Final Invitation:

Find your way to a tree you're drawn to, whether it's in your backyard, a park, or the woods, somewhere you can sit, stand, or be comfortably near it. You may want to use a chair, cushion, or blanket if that's helpful to you so you can stay for a little while.

Take some time to notice if you can see the tree's roots, the way the trunk feels, and how the light filters through the branches when you look up at them.

When you're settled, close your eyes, take a few deep breaths, and drop your awareness into your body. Maybe you want to focus on a specific place or follow your breath into your body and back out again.

Stay here for a while, noticing and allowing whatever you sense or feel.

During this time, you don't have to push away or shame your thoughts as they come and go, just gently return to sensation, to things you don't have to or can't label with words.

You don't have to think about what you're doing, just feel.

This is a chance to perceive without words, without needing to understand the story or the why. You only need to create and be in the space for yourself to be all that you are in this moment.

Acknowledgments

Nic, for helping me deepen my relationship with myself. For continuing to meet me where I am and giving me the space to be who I am. I couldn't be happier to be on this journey with you.

Grey Emerson, for showing me what it looks like to be yourself in any moment, and for all your support and love. And for reading all those drafts...yeah.

Gayle, you know all you've done and continue to do. Thank you.

Alex, working on this project with you was such a gift. Thank you for saying yes.

Nicole, for your friendship and all the writing candles.

Brandi, for your encouragement and for always embracing how I'm unfolding along the way.

Chelsea, for our voice notes, for listening to all my long, podcast-like messages, and for always being on the other end. It's amazing we haven't met in person (yet).

Sarah, for being such a constant cheerleader in my life and for all my projects.

Monique, for giving me the push I needed to begin.

And last, but certainly not least, Síomha, for your passion for bringing ease to others.

About the Author

Kay Sibson is a creative who now finds herself following what draws her in, rather than a set plan. In recent years, that has meant moving between different projects, staying open to new opportunities, and learning how to be comfortable without having all the answers.

She gravitates toward stories, especially in books and film, with a soft spot for British television and for different forms of creative expression.

She prefers deep conversations over small talk, spends a lot of time around trees, and feels most at home near the ocean, despite currently living in Montana with her family.

You can find what she's working on at www.kaysibson.com.

www.ingramcontent.com/pod-product-compliance
Lightning Source LLC
Chambersburg PA
CBHW051458130726
47987CB00005B/2372